WHEN DO YOU LET THE ANIMALS OUT?

This man can hardly contain his enthusiasm after reading this book.
Byron Harmon/Whyte Museum of the Canadian Rockies/NA-71-516

WHEN DO YOU LET THE ANIMALS OUT?

A FIELD GUIDE TO ROCKY MOUNTAIN HUMOUR

Michael Kerr

FIFTH
HOUSE
PUBLISHERS

Published by
Fifth House Ltd.
A Fitzhenry & Whiteside Company
195 Allstate Parkway
Markham, ON L3R 4T8
www.fifthhousepublishers.ca

Interior design & illustrations by Brian Smith/Articulate Eye
Cover design by Daniel Choi
Cover images courtesy of iStockphoto

Fifth House Ltd. gratefully acknowledges the support of the Canada Coun-
cil for the Arts, the Department of Canadian Heritage and the Ontario
Arts Council. We acknowledge the financial support of the Government of
Canada through the Canada Book Fund (CBF) for our publishing program.

Canada Council   Conseil des Arts
for the Arts   du Canada

ONTARIO ARTS COUNCIL
CONSEIL DES ARTS DE L'ONTARIO

This edition printed in Canada in 2011

10 9 8 7 6 5 4 3 2 1

Canadian Cataloguing in Publication Data
Kerr, Michael, 1962–
  When do you let the animals out?
(Pocket Rockies)
ISBN 978-1-92708-300-0
1. Rocky Mountains, Canadian (B.C. and Alta.)–Humour. 2. Rocky Moun-
tains, Canadian (B.C. and Alta.)–Miscellanea. I. Title. II. Series.
FC219.K495 1998   971.1'002'07   C98-910167-3
F1090.K495 1998

WHEN DO YOU LET THE ANIMALS OUT?

A FIELD GUIDE TO ROCKY MOUNTAIN HUMOUR

Acknowledgements

1 AN INTRODUCTION TO ROCKY MOUNTAIN HUMOUR 1

2 PLACES EVERYONE! 6

Did I Miss the Turnoff for Canada?

How Do I Get to Yahoo?

Every Place Tells a Story

The Rockies Place Names Challenge

3 LEAVE IT TO BEAVER—FROM THE FILES OF PARKS CANADA 23

Are You a Beaver Trainer?

In Search of a Better Beaver

Canada—Strong and Free?

Now is *That* Appropriate?

Law and Disorder

Signs You've Entered the Wrong Park

Annoying Parks Canada

Tonight's Campfire Talk—Rated R

Did I Really Say That?

Warden Highs and Woes

4 WILD LIFE AND WILD TIMES 52

When Does an Elk Become a Moose?

Watching the Wildlife Watchers Watch

Today's Mystery Animal

A Herd of Bears, a Jam of Tourists

You Are in Potato Chip Country

Jamming with the Wildlife

Snubbing Griz

Bear in Mind

Foreplay—When Golfers and Wildlife Mix

Tales of Tails in the Canadian Rockies

5 ARE YOU JUST VISITING? 100

Don't You People from Canada Know Anything?

Are You Local Enough to Live Here?

The Friendliest Visitor Letter in History

Your Guide to the Guides

Having a Good Time, Wish You Were Here

The Complete Backpacker

The Top Twenty Things to See, Do, and Smell in the Canadian Rockies

6 ON THE ROCKS 117

How Much Does that Mountain Weigh?

Geology Made Simple

A Tribute to the Little Bubnoff

Elvis Has Left the Park

Climbing the Walls

7 A HYSTERICAL HISTORY OF
THE ROCKIES 131

The First Silly Visitor Questions and Comments

Humour in the Rockies: The Early Years

A Chronology of Rocky Mountain Humour

Don't Quote Me

Yesterday's News

8 THE WILDERNESS ZONE 149

The Last of the Silly Questions and Comments

Mountain-Grown Corn

Impractical Practical Jokes in the Rockies

Saturday Night Beaver

The Jurassic Park Cattle Guard

Sex in the Rockies

The Chinook Made Me Do It

An Elmer Fudd Theme Park?

Is that a Hairy Chested Nut-Scratcher?

Hollywood Comes to the Rockies

Ten Reasons Waterton Lakes Isn't Mentioned More
Often in this Book

And Now, The News . . .

The Great Canadian Rockies Quiz

ACKNOWLEDGEMENTS

No field guide containing this much fluff could have been prepared by one person. I had conspirators.

I'd like to thank the following for their generous assistance: Parks Canada, The Whyte Museum of the Canadian Rockies, The Banff *Crag and Canyon*, The Jasper *Booster,* and the Banff–Lake Louise Tourism Bureau. Thanks also to the staff of the Banff Visitor Centre, Two Jack Campground, Lake Louise Visitor Centre, Yoho Visitor Centre, Columbia Icefield Centre, and Jasper Visitor Centre for their contributions to the silly questions.

For their time and/or contributions (if your story isn't here, don't panic, we're just waiting for volume II, or conversely we could blame it on the editor) I'd like to thank the following: Tim Auger, Gordon Burles, Mary Coleman, Keith Everts, Larry Halverson, Gord Irwin, Helen Kennedy, Gloria Keyes-Brady, Sean Krausert, Art Lawrence, Ron Leblanc, Claude Lemieux, Elaine Lemieux, Phil Lewis, Felix Lighter, Michelle Macullo, Locke Marshall, Don Mickle, Ann Morrow, Glen Peers, Dale Portman, Cyndi Smith, George Smith, Janice Smith, Jim Takenaka, Mark Tierney, Rob Tooke, Scot Ward, Mark Whelan, and Brad White. (If some of you don't remember contributing, it's okay, I probably eavesdropped or just rifled through your notes when you weren't looking.) If I missed anyone please accept my apologies and my gratitude.

I'd also like to express my appreciation for the anonymous contributions from waitresses, taxi drivers, bartenders, shepherds, and chiropractors. I'd like to thank them, but since they chose to remain anonymous, there's not a damned thing I can do about it.

A special thanks to Brian Patton, who not only introduced me to a whole new line of "writer's distractions" but also kindly offered much help throughout the project, and to Claudine Dumais, who reviewed the first drafts and offered invaluable comments (so now you know why the odd French word has slipped in).

Finally, a book like this could only be achieved with a faithful dog at your side. Thanks, Eeyore, for your constant, well, just lying around at my feet, and for not freaking out when I spilled coffee on my printer.

A final thanks to the folks at Fifth House Publishers for buying me lunch last summer and for their continuous support throughout the project.

Michael Kerr and Eeyore. *Claudine Dumais*

AN INTRODUCTION TO ROCKY MOUNTAIN HUMOUR

So What Is Rocky Mountain Humour, Anyway?

Mountain humour's home range extends throughout mountainous terrain. It is, quite simply, humour that pertains to a mountainish theme. It is a distinctive tenor of humour that can be found only where people spend too much time at high elevations. As we all know, there is less oxygen at higher altitudes, and the brain does strange things when deprived of oxygen. It stops working properly. It makes sense, then, that there would be a distinctive brand of jocularity known as mountain humour that is decidedly different than, say, polar ice pack

humour. And certainly different than lunar or jungle humour, and strikingly unique when compared to deep sea humour.

This field guide covers the mountain humour indigenous to the Canadian Rockies, which has a different flavour than that of the American Rockies to the south or the Columbia Mountains to the west. In fact, as we shall see, the Columbia Mountains tend to take themselves far too seriously and should really lighten up a little.

Where Does Rocky Mountain Humour Originate?

Generally, in the Rocky Mountains.

Within the Rocky Mountains we find recurring themes. The wildlife is a constant source of humour, usually because of the things we do with it, to it, or because of it. The national parks—Banff in particular—also provide a wealth of possibilities. I make no apologies for the Banffocentric approach in this book. The reality is that strange things are more likely to happen in Banff simply because Banff is Banff. It's sort of the Disneyland of the national park system. Goofy things tend to happen there.

And, of course, we could not focus on Canadian Rockies humour without referring to Parks Canada. Parks Canada is the landlord of a large chunk of these mountains and is thus responsible for much of the humorous goings-on in them. Without Parks Canada, bless its little heart, things would be a lot duller around here.

Finally, much humour is provided by *homo sapiens mucholosto*—park visitors. Remember, these people are in a strange land, far from home, often meeting wildlife and wilderness for the first time. Something has to give.

A Few Words about Silly Questions

Our visitors say a lot of silly things while they're here, which is why all the chapters begin with a section of silly questions and comments. But before you run to the publisher screaming in outrage, do keep this in mind: we are laughing *with* them, not *at* them. (Except for that fellow from Ohio; we were definitely laughing *at* him.) Visitors enjoy silly questions as much as the locals do (they must; they ask enough of them) and most of them realize the silliness of their question as soon as they've asked it. They laugh at themselves before anyone else has a chance to. Besides, we *all* know we're capable of asking such questions ourselves. Even *moi*. While on a recent train ride to Churchill, Manitoba, I asked the server in the dining car if it was water or the open tundra I was looking at. She placed my breakfast before me and calmly explained that what I was looking at was the sky.

I'm a firm believer in the old saying, "There are no silly questions, only silly answers, and silly hats." In other words, silly questions are acceptable (even encouraged; we may do a second volume of this book), but silly answers are not. So, when reading the questions, think of them as a celebration of our natural curiosity and innocence in a strange land rather than a reflection on the people themselves—except, of course, for that one guy from Ohio.

The questions were passed on to me from a number of sources. Parks Canada contributed many, as did tourism bureaus, travel agents, bus drivers, guides, meeting planners, waitresses, bartenders, taxi drivers, and chiropractors—in other words, just about anyone who has ever encountered a visitor in the Canadian Rockies.

How To Use this Book

This book may be used as a paper weight, to train your black lab to fetch, or to assess your posture while walking back and forth like royalty. If all else fails, it may also be read. It can be read from start to finish, dipped into at random, or read upside down and backwards while lying in a tent. Some of the stories are actually funnier if you read them this way. But don't try it at home. It only works in a tent.

Like any good field guide, this book is designed to be given to friends—especially those you're not particularly fond of. Alternatively, you can stuff it into some obscure corner of a rarely used book shelf. The importance of this strategy is twofold: first, you've purchased the book, and second, you've added to your shelf space, thus propagating the myth that you are a well-read person.

I would strongly recommend, however, that, as with any field guide, you carry it with you at all times. It is designed to be small enough to be carried with you while backpacking, hiking, birding, mammaling, and attending cocktail parties, the opera, or a hockey game. If you have to visit the rest room while dining out, take the book with you. If, God forbid, you are in an accident, make sure the book is on your person. You never know when you'll need it, and you'll look all the more foolish for not having it handy.

Imagine, for example, that you're driving down the highway and one of your children cuts through the silence with, "Hey, Daddy, tell us something funny that has a mountain theme to it." Without this guide you'd be lost. Or imagine sitting at the bar and one of your pals asks if anyone's heard any good porcupine jokes lately. Without this guide, you'll be caught red-faced and with your pants down. Without this guide, in fact, you will not only be unable to initiate mountain humour, you won't know how to identify it when you see or hear it. Then where will you be?

Who Is this Guide For?

Anyone with a love of the mountains, a desire to poke fun at Parks Canada, or who is just really really bored. Do you have to be a local to appreciate it? Of course not. Some of the fun is definitely inside humour (you have to be inside my brain to think it's amusing), and a few references may require some insider knowledge of the mountains, Parks Canada, or the reproductive cycle of marmots. So if something doesn't strike you as amusing, don't feel bad, you're just probably not very knowledgeable about marmots.

What's In this Guide?

Like any field guide, this book has pages, words, and chapters. The chapters cover the following topics: place names of the Rockies, Parks Canada, wildlife, tourists, geology, history, and a hodgepodge category for the things that are too asinine to fit anywhere else. Each chapter begins with silly visitor questions and goes downhill from there.

Unlike other field guides, there are no confusing distribution maps, detailed field marks, obscure scientific jargon, and none of that annoying concern with things such as details and accuracy.

So dive in and enjoy the swim. And for God's sake, if you're reading this in the mountains, please don't feed the chipmunks.

PLACES EVERYONE!

DID I MISS THE TURNOFF FOR CANADA?

So many highways, so many directions, so many names, so few signs . . .

It's clear from the following questions and comments that many of our visitors have trouble getting a sense of place. In fact, many of them can't even *find* their place . . .

From the "I Think I Might Be Lost" Files

Did I miss the turnoff for Canada?

How far to the Canadian Rockies? (Asked in Lake Louise, Field, Banff, and Canmore.)

Are we in Saskatchewan yet?

Are we in Manitoba yet?

Is this the part of Canada where they speak a lot of French, or is that Saskatchewan?

If I take the road with the sign that says Lake Louise, will that get me to Jasper?

Is there any way out of here?

Can you tell me where we're going?

Where *are* we going, anyway?

Don't give me any directions, just point.

Where did I just come from?

> VISITOR: Is Moraine Lake actually Lake Louise?
> INFORMATION STAFF: No, it's actually Moraine Lake.
> VISITOR: Oh.

Which way are we headed, you ask? Gosh, I could never figure out where we are!

Did I just come from Jasper?

If I go out, will I get lost?

How many roads can you get lost on?

Where does Alberta end and Canada begin?

Can we visit a part of Canada that Canadians haven't seen yet?

We're leaving Lake Louise for Banff town. Once we get to Banff, how do we get to Lake Louise?

If I turn right, is that the fastest way to Seattle?

You people have a conspiracy with your highway

When they leave home, they don't know where they're going; when they get there, they don't know where they are; and when they get back home, they don't know where they've been.

—THE LATE JIMMY SIMPSON, LEGENDARY GUIDE AND OUTFITTER, ON HOW TOURISTS ARE A LOT LIKE CHRISTOPHER COLUMBUS signs to mix people up so we stay longer and spend more money!

Do you have maps of the United States? No? How about the northern United States?

If I go to Kelowna, do I have to go back to Ontario the same way?

Is this a map I'm looking at?

Do you have a map of Jasper state?

Can I have a map of New Mexico, please?

How far to the Arctic Circle?

Is this map *just* for Alaska? (Pointing to a map of Jasper National Park.)

Is Banff a town, a park, a mountain . . . just *what* the heck is it, and *where* is it?*

Where do we start and where do we finish?

I was here an hour ago and was told the road to Jasper was straight, so why am I back here?

> VISITOR: Can I have a map?
> ATTENDANT: Sure, where are you going?
> VISITOR: I'm not going anywhere.

Can you tell me what lies beyond?

If I get lost, how will I find my way again?

There's no way out of this park is there?

HOW DO I GET TO YAHOO?

Considerably more difficult than finding one's place in the Rockies, is pronouncing its name properly. Of course, this makes sense. We have people from all over the world trying to say these names for the first time. And we don't make it easy for them. Banff. Yoho. Athabasca Glacier. Minnewanka Lake. Takakkaw Falls. Maligne Lake. The only place name in the Rockies I've never heard anyone

---

* Banff is a town, a park, and, believe it or not, a crater on Mars. This means when Martians start visiting, things will get even more confusing.

mess up is Boom Lake. So, in honour of some of our more common tongue twisting monikers (gosh, I love the word "moniker"), I present the following from our "trying their best" visitor files.

The Top Ten Ways Not to Say Banff *

10. Barnff	5. Vamp
9. Banffffffff	4. Baffin
8. Bannnnnf	3. Branff
7. Bann-if	2. Bannock
6. Buff	1. Banff-fuh-fuh**

You Who! Over Here!

Yoho is a Cree word meaning "wonder" or "awe." There are two other possibilities, however, both of which just occurred to me. One is that the original name of the park was "You Who" after two explorers who, on being separated, were heard calling out, "You who! I'm over here!" The other possibility is that the true meaning of Yoho was watered down over the years and really means "Holy shit, this place is incredible!"

But I digress. Here are the top ten ways *not* to say Yoho. (If you say them fast enough, it sounds like a visit to the Calgary Stampede.)

10. Yahoo!	5. Coho
9. Yoho***	4. Oyo
8. Yolo	3. Yeehaw
7. Yoyo	2. Yaha
6. Hoyo	1. You-Who!

---

* Someone once told me, "To pronounce Banff correctly you have to sound like you're passing a little gas at the end of the word, it's all in the 'phuh' at the end." But by far the easiest—and correct—way to pronounce it is "Ban-ph."

** Talk show host David Lettermen once pronounced Banff this way, although I think he did it on purpose to irk us.

*** Wait a minute, that *is* how you pronounce Yoho.

Of course, one of the highlights of Yahoo National Park is Takakkaw Falls. Did I say Takakkaw? Sorry, I meant Tick-a-cow . . .

> Tick-a-tock?
>
> Taka-taka-taka?
>
> Ticky ticky?
>
> Tacabacca?
>
> Takakaka?
>
> Taka . . . take a . . . taka . . . oh, forget it.

Would the Real Icefields Parkway Please Stand Up?

Could I please have some information on the . . .

Icecold highway?	Ice gardens?
Snowmobile parkway?	Iceshields parkway?
Iceberg parkway?	Icefields city?
Ice cube highway?	Bow medicine parkway?
Iceland trail?	Snowmo-fields parkway?
Icefloes parkway?	Ice Atlantique highway?
Icelandic highway?	Iceway parkway?

. . . and include some information on the . . .

Columbia icepack	Columbian icebergs
Columbian rice fields	Columbian icicles
Columbian icelands	Cambrian iceshields

. . . and while we're at the Columbia Icefields, could you be sure to point out the Athabasca glacier, or rather the . . .

Athabasca oilfields	Abscam glacier
Athenia glacier	Alablah glacier
Athabasca icicle	Athabastard glacier
Askabatha glacier	Abbagabba glacier
ABBA glacier	Tabasco glacier

Athabathka glacier (Yeth, yeth, we thertainly could point that out)

Sometimes it can take some effort to get to the answer we are looking for:

> *Visitor:* How do you pronounce Athabasca falls? Does it start with Asta?
> *Information Staff:* Atha.
> *Visitor:* Agga?
> *Staff:* Atha.
> *Visitor:* Amma?
> *Staff:* Atha.
> *Visitor:* Atha?
> *Staff:* Atha.
> *Visitor:* Oh, you mean like the glacier, Athabasca!

Final Jeopardy

Clearly, the previous locales win the prize for the most frequently mangled, garbled, and maimed place names. But there are lots more to come . . .

What Was Asked For	*The Answer We Were Hoping to Get*
Casper National Park	Jasper National Park
Mount Edith Gazelle	Mount Edith Cavell
Plato Lake	Peyto Lake
Sasquatch Crossing	Saskatchewan Crossing
Sasquathchewan Crossing	
Koot-en-annie	Kootenay National Park
Koot-in-ninnie	
Radiation Hot Springs	Radium Hot Springs
Nuclear Hot Springs	
Rapido Hot Springs	
Radon Hot Spring	
Uranium Hot Springs	
Lake Lousie	Lake Louise
Lake St. Louis	
Lake Louisiana	

Tea House of the August Moon	Lake Agnes Tea House
Lake Agnes Soup Kitchen	
Lake Agnes Tree House	
Honeycomb Hut	
Morainey Lake	Moraine Lake
Marmoraine Lake	
Boring Lake	
Moron Lake	
Morphine Lake	
Valley of the 10,000 Smokes	Valley of the Ten Peaks
Valley of the 12 Apostles	
Valley of the Thousand Peaks	
Valley of the Hundred Peaks	
Valley of the Twenty Dollar Bill*	
Cancellation Lakes	Consolation Lakes
Consolidation Lakes	
Kissing Horse	Kicking Horse River
Kinky Horse	
Hungry Horse	
Crazy Tunnels	Spiral Tunnels
Corkscrew Tunnels	
Voodoo campground	Hoodoo campground
Lake Minnie-wanky	Lake Minnewanka
Two Bob Lake	Two Jack Lake
Three Jacks Lake	
Jack and Jack Lake	

* The old Canadian twenty-dollar bill featured Moraine Lake and the Valley of the Ten Peaks. The new twenty has a couple of loons on it (three if you count Queen Elizabeth, but I wouldn't if I were you). Naturally, some visitors ask the locals to show them to the lake where the two loons are, hoping to see Moraine Lake with the two loons swimming on it.

Mt. Rumble	Mt. Rundle
The Yahoos	The Hoodoos
The Hobos	
The Voodoos	
Mount Ass n' bone	Mount Assiniboine

EVERY PLACE TELLS A STORY

In his book *The Buffalo Head*, R. M. Patterson opines that "the Rockies must surely be the worst named mountain range in the world." He may be right. We have some very strange names that reveal nothing of either the landscape

We used the word "Banffite" in a headline last week for the first time since we came here. We've sort of shied away from using it up to now mainly because it brings to mind similar-sounding words like gelignite, dynamite and other blasted or blasting terms.

We have not found Banff residents to be of a particularly explosive nature so far, although doubtless it is just a question of time before we print SOMETHING that displeases SOME local resident, whereupon we will find out that Banffites can be very explosive indeed.

Actually, "Banffites" is probably as good a term as anything else and certainly a whole lot better than Haligonians, which is the term under which residents of Halifax labour.

We could go on and on with this subject, of course.

The name "Banffibians" has a pleasant lilt to it, but unfortunately calls to mind such things as frogs, turtles and salamanders, et cetera, and we think it unlikely that our townspeople would want to be associated with these fauna.

BANFF *CRAG AND CANYON*, APRIL 23, 1958

Everyone working at high altitudes invariably ends up dressing like the wildlife. *Michael Kerr*

or of local history. And beyond some of the mismatched monikers, we're not even sure that some of the mountains bear the names they were originally christened with. There was a lot of "We *think* he meant this mountain, but we're not sure" going on when the bureaucrats took over. Okay, so maybe some of our mountains sound as if they were named by a bunch of drunken politicians (many of the better ones *were* picked this way), but we still have our great looks.

If only our explorers and mapmakers had had one of those baby-naming books—*1,001 Names for Your Baby Mountain*, say—*then* we'd have some good mountain names: Destiny Ridge, the Eiger II, Kilimanjaro Jr., Spencer, Matthew, Sarah, and Ashley.

Or imagine if our landmarks had been named by the folks who labelled the sport climbing routes (see Chapter 6 for a truly breathtaking list of silly names). Banff might lie in the shadow of *Dr. Gilligan's House of Earwax*, while Moraine Lake could be cradled in the *Valley of the Ten Pregnant Monkeys*. Castle Mountain would naturally be the *Castle of the Surfing Zombies*, while Mount Edith

Cavell would become *Mount Edith and Archie Bunker*. Kicking Horse Pass would be *Kicking Ass Pass*, while the Bears Hump in Waterton Lakes might be . . . well, let's not go there, shall we?

The good place names, of course, have stories behind them. The better names have stories that may or may not be true, while the best place names have stories that probably aren't true but we'd like to believe they are. Here are a few examples of some of the stranger stories behind our beloved Canadian Rockies place names (and they are all absolutely true).

Lake Agnes

Cradled in a valley high above Lake Louise, Lake Agnes honours the wife of our first Prime Minister, Sir John A. Macdonald. Lady Susan Agnes Macdonald hiked up to the lake one day in the fall of 1890, supposedly the first white woman to visit the lake. Willoughby J. Astley, manager of the Lake Louise Chalet, however, claimed that the first woman to have seen the lake was a Miss Agnes Knox, and that the lake was named for *her*. On finding this out, Lady Macdonald gracefully decided to allow the name to stand, as her middle name was fortunately Agnes—a small coincidence that settled what could have been an awful bloody mess.

Banff

The official version is that Banff, the town and park, derive their name from Banff, Scotland, the home of two early Canadian Pacific Railway directors. Historian Brian Patton, however, suggests that the name may also come from the word *Banb*, the goddess of swine. (Gee, thanks, Brian, we'll stick with the original version.)

Bath Creek

This creek near the Banff-Yoho border was named by Tom Wilson, a guide and outfitter, after the cranky surveyor Major A. B. Rogers fell into the creek while crossing it in the early 1880s. Rogers claimed it was "the first bath he had taken all summer." Later, whenever the creek

turned cloudy with silt, his men would joke, "The Major must be taking another bath." Were they a bunch of kidders, or what?

Bertha Peak and Lake

These two Berthas are located near the town of Waterton in Waterton Lakes National Park. The name honours Bertha Eklund, an early settler. Her boyfriend, a mountain man named Joe Cosley, named the peak and lake in her honour. Bertha was later jailed for passing counterfeit money, while Joe was arrested for poaching, which only goes to show that, if you were around early enough, anyone could get a place named after them.

Castle Mountain

Dr. James Hector of the 1858 Palliser Expedition reportedly looked up at this mountain and said, "Looks kind of like a castle. Hey, how about calling it Castle Mountain?" Of course, someone had to come along later and screw up one of the most straightforward names in the Rockies. That someone was the federal government. (Hard to believe, isn't it?)

Following World War II, Scotland had given Dwight D. Eisenhower a castle to express its thanks for the general's war efforts. Following Scotland's lead, Prime Minister

Mackenzie King decided to rename Castle Mountain in the general's honour. (It was much cheaper just to rename a castle than give one to him.) The mountain was officially Mount Eisenhower from 1945 to 1979, when the feds decided to reinstate the original name. The first peak, however, still retains the name Eisenhower. Tour bus drivers have been known to call the meadow below the peak "Eisenhower's Putting Green" to memorialize the rumour that Eisenhower was too busy golfing to attend the official naming ceremony in his honour.

Disaster Point

Before disco and the railway, the lower cliffs of Roche Miette stuck out like a sore thumb into the Athabasca River. This protrusion forced early explorers either to ford the river or make an arduous detour around the entire bloody thing. Naturally, many accidents befell parties trying to navigate past the obstruction. You would expect, then, that the "disaster" in Disaster Point refers to a truly horrifying, disastrous trip. And you would be right. The point was christened after the Reverend George Grant and the CPR engineer Sanford Fleming travelled up the valley on September 1, 1872. The Reverend Grant documented the appalling episode:

It had been a day long to be remembered. Only one mishap occurred: the Chief's bag got a crush against a rock, and his flask, that held a drop of brandy carefully preserved for the next plum-pudding, was broken. It was hard, but on an expedition like this the most serious losses are taken calmly and soon forgotten.

Fernie

The town of Fernie, nestled (why are mountain towns always "nestled"?) in the southern Rockies along the Crowsnest Pass, was not named, as some have suggested, "because it's very ferny in the forests around there." The name honours William Fernie, who discovered coal in the region in 1887, and later became director of the Coal Creek Mine. The Kootenay Indians, however, have a less flattering story to relate.

Allegedly, Mr. Fernie promised to marry a young Kootenay woman in return for information about the region's coal deposits. After Fernie discovered the coal, he abandoned the woman. The woman's mother was outraged and called on the spirits to place a curse upon Fernie and his town. The curse may have worked. In 1902, 128 men died in the Coal Creek Mine, while in 1904 and 1908 much of the town was destroyed by fire.

The Kootenay nation held a ceremony in 1964 to remove the curse from the town. Since then, the only reported disaster was in 1974 when the mayor was badly constipated for three weeks.

Mount Fifi

This rugged peak just west of Banff is likely the only mountain in the Rockies named after a French poodle. It was christened by surveyor Louis B. Stewart, following a hike over Edith Pass with Ms Edith Orde and her dog, Fifi. Cute, eh? Imagine being a mountain climber and having to say you're "Off to conquer Fifi today" or "Think I'll bag Fifi." It's embarrassing.

Lake Louise

Lake Louise is named for the daughter of Queen Victoria, Princess Louise Caroline Alberta. The princess is also the reason Alberta is named Alberta and not, say, Rex or Scamper, or even Fifi. The princess never visited Lake Louise. (Being a princess, she probably did whatever she damned well pleased.)

There is a more romantic version. According to this account, the lake was named by the first white person to see it, guide and outfitter Tom Wilson. Tom was led to the lake in 1882 by Stoney Indians, who knew it as the Lake of Little Fishes (anglers have subsequently claimed that they actually called it the Lake of Really, Really Little Fishes). Tom originally called it Emerald Lake, but he renamed it after taking Sir Richard Temple (of the British Association for the Advancement of Science) and his daughter to see the lake. Tom, being the old smoothie that he was, changed the lake's name to honour Sir Richard's daughter. (This, of course, is one of the oldest tricks in the book, much older than running out of gas. I would have tried it several times myself had everything not been already named.)

Mosquito Creek

This creek along the Icefields Parkway was named after someone ran into several billion mosquitoes there. (What did you think?) The Mosquito Creek Campground was named by the same marketing geniuses that brought us squeezable cheese and sea monkeys.

Redstreak Canyon

Located in the southernmost part of Kootenay National Park, Redstreak Canyon is named for the vein of iron oxide in the rocks. Of course, the locals have alternative theories. Some claim the canyon is named for the abundance of mosquitoes in the area, and the red streaks they leave on your arm after you've swatted them. Others say it's named because someone streaked in the area (at least one person actually did, but whether he was red or not is a matter for debate). In any case, geologists assure us that, as iron oxide weathers, it becomes brown, so eventually the canyon will have to be renamed Brownstreak—and a whole new set of possibilities will present itself.

St. Nicholas Peak

This peak was apparently named after jolly old St. Nick because a rock formation near the top looks like Santa Claus. (Yeah, right—if you've been into the whiskey and look at the peak during a blinding snowstorm.)

Tunnel Mountain

Everyone asks where the tunnel is, and rightfully so. There is no tunnel. It's hard to imagine what was going through someone's mind: "Hmmm, I think I'll name this Tunnel Mountain because there's no tunnel going through it." The mountain—the smallest in Banff

National Park, an embarrassment, really—was named after an early CPR survey conducted by Major A. B. Rogers called for a tunnel through it. Fortunately, surveyor Charles Shaw looked on the other side of the mountain and realized the silliness of this idea. As Shaw said in his memoirs, "Rogers' location here was the most extraordinary blunder I have ever known in the way of engineering." The route was altered to avoid the mountain, but the name stuck. In the interests of eliminating the confusion, a coalition of interested parties (PAC-MAN: People Against Confusing Monikers and Names) is currently lobbying to have a tunnel blasted through the mountain.

THE ROCKIES PLACE NAMES CHALLENGE

1. The *Valley of the Ten Peaks* is so named because . . .
   a) there are fourteen peaks in the area
   b) *Valley of the Dolls* was already being used
   c) *Valley of the One Peak* didn't sound substantial enough

2. The *Bears Hump* in Waterton . . .
   a) is the name of a small hill overlooking Waterton where bears go to mess around
   b) as often as they can
   c) so be particularly cautious while hiking in the Waterton Lakes area

3. *Canmore* is named after . . .
   a) a famous Scot who coined the term "exponential growth"
   b) the Air Farce character, "Mike from Canmore," who got really drunk before the naming committee's first meeting
   c) no obvious or relevant person or thing because the committee couldn't think of one

4. *Jasper* town is named for . . .
   a) the fun of it
   b) Jasper the Bear, the town mascot (the mascot was actually created first, in hopes it would necessitate the building of a town)
   c) Jasper, the 8th dwarf, who died in a tragic mining accident

5. *Mud Lake* near Lake Louise is so named because . . .
   a) it's a lake, so Mud *Creek* would be rather silly
   b) local businesses wanted to attract more tourists to its scenic shoreline
   c) it's where they hold those monster truck shows

6. The *North Saskatchewan River* is named the North Saskatchewan River because . . .
   a) everything needs a name, otherwise we'd just call it "that river"
   b) we enjoy making tourists believe they have to pass through Saskatchewan *en route* to Jasper
   c) the headwaters of the river are in Alberta

7. A common nickname for the *Continental Divide* is . . .
   a) the Continental Breakfast Served On High*
   b) the pelvis of the North American continent
   c) that really, really, high place that divides the flow of water in two directions
   d) the Sultan of all Divides

8. The *Devil's Gap* at the end of Lake Minnewanka in Banff is so named because . . .
   a) Satan once went fishing there and got pissed off because he didn't catch his limit
   b) the *Angel's Crack* didn't sound foreboding enough
   c) it sounds really scary, and thus keeps small children away

9. The *Columbia Icefield* is so named because . . .
   a) it's *not* the headwaters of the Columbia River
   b) it's *not* the headwaters of the Columbia River
   c) look, it's *really not* the headwaters of the Columbia River; everyone just thinks it is
   d) all of the above

10. The *Three Sisters* peaks overlooking Canmore are named after . . .
    a) three nuns who got lost while climbing the back side of the first peak
    b) the characters from *Charlie's Angels*
    c) a soul band whose tour bus broke down in the vicinity

* I know, this really doesn't make any sort of sense. It just seems really stupid now that I look at it, but I'm a little cranky right now, so let's just leave it alone.

LEAVE IT TO BEAVER– FROM THE FILES OF PARKS CANADA

ARE YOU A BEAVER TRAINER?

More questions, comments, and insights from our beloved guests, this time on the subject of Parks Canada:

> Is the campground interpretive program compulsory?
>
> Does my park permit pay for my gas while I'm travelling in the park?
>
> Is there entertainment in this campground for my kids? No, no, not a naturalist program, you know . . . pinball, pool tables, that kind of thing.
>
> Are you a beaver trainer? (Gesturing to the beaver logo on a Parks Canada employee's uniform.)
>
> Warden, huh? Is that the same as a prison warden?
>
> How many languages do you park interpreters speak?
>
> Do women need a park fishing licence?*
>
> Does Parks Canada issue painting permits for artists?
>
> Can I use my vehicle sticker to fish with?**
>
> Do they shoot you if you don't renew your park pass?

---

* Women are free to move about the park without any special permits or licences—just thought I'd clear that up.
** Only if you wrap a worm around it. (I'm kidding. There's no live bait allowed in national parks.)

I've got my park entrance permit, now where's the damned entrance?

So what do you parks people call yourselves these days?

Is Parks Canada a Canadian thing or what?

Is the park permit free if you're not planning on buying anything?

IN SEARCH OF A BETTER BEAVER

Cutbacks have hit Parks Canada so badly that they've had to downgrade their official logo from a beaver to a muskrat.

But seriously, Parks Canada *is* looking for a new beaver (and really, who isn't?). They even surveyed folks

to begin the quest for a better, stronger beaver. I decided to conduct my own survey, in order to help out in my own small way. One summer weekend I asked more than 100 campers the following question: "What does this logo look like to you?" The results prove either that a new beaver really *is* needed, or that our campers need help, and they need it quickly.

Survey #1: What Does This Parks Logo Look Like to You?

A pork chop	Elvis (the later years)*
A vole	A map of District West**

---

* Try this at home kids—turn the beaver logo on its side and it really does look like Elvis.

** This response from a Parks Canada employee refers to a new administrative unit, but to explain it would take up far too much space. It will be treated thoroughly in an upcoming book entitled *101 Ways to Confuse the Public, Your Staff, and Yourself.*

A mouse	A bear or cow do-do
A squid	An otter
Snoopy	A squirrel
An angry beaver	A hound dog
A duck	A chipmunk
A backed-over beaver	My baby brother
A spleen	A pancake
A tailless beaver	A beagle
An island off Maine	A bison

The Rude Beaver

"Park Officials Find Sticker Too Rude" read the headline in the Calgary *Herald*, reporting on the case of the copycat beaver stickers. The owners of a Banff business, *The Rude Boys Ski, Surf, and Shred Shop*, printed up humorous stickers resembling the Parks Canada permit, with the labels changed to read Snowboard Canada and Rude Service instead of Environment Canada and Park Service, respectively. In place of the lone "R" indicating a resident's permit, the Rude Boys placed, naturally, the word RUDE. They hoped to sell the stickers for $2, a steal compared to the normal $30 park fee for an annual pass.

Their attempt at humour unfortunately didn't wash with Parks Canada officials, who were concerned about trademark infringement and the fact that someone might be laughing at them without their knowledge. The Mounties got their man (or in this case, their beaver), seizing and destroying 350 stickers—the largest recorded beaver bust in Canadian history.

For some truly expert advice I consulted thirty three- and four-year-olds at a pre-school (much cheaper than image consultants) and got the following responses:

A chicken	A fish
A snake	A seal
A rhino	A racoon
A slug	A tap dance shoe
A bear	A puppy
A skunk	A monkey
A frog	A bee
A worm	A chipmunk
A butterfly	A beaver
A bird	A triangle
A mouse	A polar bear

Survey #2: What Should the New Parks Canada Logo Be?

Then I asked the following: "Okay, what *should* the new Parks Canada logo be?" I weeded out the serious suggestions, which were *far* too serious to be taken lightly, and was left with the following suggestions:

A dollar sign

A motor home

A maple leaf with a disease

A half-eaten beaver

A mounted beaver (to show how parks is getting . . .)

A mounted policeman (don't go there)

A more macho beaver

An under construction symbol

A no parking symbol

A hockey stick

An elk

Mickey Mouse

A dinosaur

"Mmmm . . . either a lion or a bat"*

CANADA—
STRONG AND FREE?

Your entrance fee into the national parks helps pay for the protection of the park and the facilities that you, the park visitor, might want to use. (Of course, if you do use them, you'll have to pay for that, too.) The park entrance permit system has, thank goodness, become simpler over the years. Remember when you had to pay a flat fee per vehicle for the entire year? It was a complicated, confusing, and time-wasting procedure. Now things are much more straightforward.

In May 1996, a couple from Saskatchewan had their car broken into while visiting Jasper. The thief ignored several valuable items, taking the only item of any *real* value —their park permit.

---

* This came from a four-year-old named Ryan, who had a better grasp of the issue than most adults I talked to.

The Proposed New Parks Canada Fee Schedule

Please circle the following choices to determine your park fee:

Length of Stay	*Number in Group*
Less than 5 minutes	1
Maybe a couple of hours	2
1 day, tops	3
2 days	We're more of a "clan"
Odd # days	We live together but we're not married
Even # days	We're not even sleeping together
Unlimited access during night hours	>100
Unlimited access on Tuesdays	
Unlimited access in April & November	

Parks You'll Be Visiting	*Number of Left-Handed People in Group*
1	<5
2 or more	>1
Elk Island, Baffin Island, & Yoho*	I'm ambidextrous, does that count?
Parks beginning with the letters G-M	
Do we have to?	

Do You Plan on Consuming Any Oxygen?

❐ Yes   ❐ No   ❐ I'll wait and see

---

* This is the special Mountain Madness Value Package—your best deal.

Another happy camper off to enjoy the Canadian wilderness.
Michael Kerr

NOW, IS THAT *APPROPRIATE?*

To help protect our national treasures, Parks Canada has guidelines that dictate what is, and more importantly, what *is not* appropriate inside our parks. This ensures that things like nude bungee jumping, square dancing, monster truck shows, and Tommy Hunter concerts will never be allowed inside our national parks. The following chart should help clarify what constitutes an appropriate activity in our mountain national parks:

Appropriate	*Inappropriate*
Soaking in the hot springs	Peeing in the hot springs
Hiking	Dancing the Macarena
Cross country skiing	Bobsledding
Camping in a designated campground	Camping on a wildlife overpass
Asking where a good hiking trail is	Asking where the nearest K-mart is
Catch and release fishing	Catch and release hunting

An example of appropriate behaviour inside our parks.
Whyte Museum of the Canadian Rockies/NA 66-66

Wildlife watching	Looking in people's RVs while they sleep
Mountain climbing	Climbing the malls in downtown Banff
Canoeing, kayaking	Cruise ship excursions
Owning a Tilley hat	Actually putting it on your head
Mountain biking	Mountain tricycling
Attending naturalist programs	Attending naturist programs*
Driving for pleasure	Driving for the express purpose of pissing off other drivers

LAW AND DISORDER

Park regulations help protect the park from the people, and people from other people. Although some would argue there are too many regulations, I, for one, would

---

* Let's clear this up right now: a naturalist is someone who studies natural history, a naturist is someone who walks around naked, generally with other people who are also walking around naked. Although some naturalists enjoy being naked, it is not a prerequisite for the job.

like to see more added to make life a little easier on the rest of us.

Desperately Needed Park Regulations

214 – C – section 5.5: The wearing of identical outfits by bird-watching couples will not be permitted inside national park boundaries.

404 – D – section 1.7: Operators of motor homes will no longer be permitted to drive them inside a national park until the driver has demonstrated proficiency in one of the following:

a) operating a train locomotive
b) piloting a cruise ship
c) flying the space shuttle

515 – A – section 1.4: Motorists who stop in the middle of the Trans-Canada Highway to observe wildlife will be escorted out of the park and given a one-way bus ticket to Toronto and enrolled in a remedial driver education program.

666 – section 2.5: Parks Canada managers will no longer be permitted to reply in a media interview:

a) "We're still looking at all the options."
b) "We'll let you know as soon as we know."
c) "We're going to study that for the next seventeen years."

Officials caught violating this order will be required to read the book *Media Relations Secrets*, by Brian Mulroney.

890 – section 101.4: People caught videotaping while operating a motor vehicle must undergo a battery of psychiatric tests and watch *America's Funniest Home Videos* for a period of no less than twenty-four consecutive hours.

101 – section 6: Campers who insist on singing campfire songs while swaying back and forth and holding hands will be required to spend at least two weeks confined with Mr. Rogers.

454 – section 12: Visitors caught feeding junk food to park wildlife will be forced to taste test my home cooking for a period of no less than one week.

555 – section 14.1: Any visitor caught approaching bears will be required to watch *The Edge*, an adventure movie co-starring Bart the man-eating grizzly.

SIGNS YOU'VE ENTERED THE WRONG PARK

The park mascot is a giant liver fluke.

The campground has hook-up and hook-er sections.

There are no hot springs, only "kinda lukewarm springs."

The only warning signs read: "Do Not Approach or Feed Other Campers."

The campground is located on an abandoned drive-in site.

Rabid environmentalists terrorize hikers, causing trail closures.

The only guide book available is the *Field Guide to the Mosquitoes*.

Campers are not permitted to stay overnight in the campgrounds.

The toothless Chief Park Warden, a man named "Bubba," enjoys catching flower pickers . . . far away from the road . . . alone. (Look, do I have to spell it out for you?)

The only call of the wild is coming from the tent at campsite D-12.

The first billboard along a scenic drive reads: "Do *You* Have An Updated Rabies Shot?"

Campfire programs carry nudity and coarse language warnings.

Picnic sites include a complementary jar of ants.

Poking fun at Parks Canada is a time-honoured Canadian tradition, as this anonymous letter to the editor proves. It appeared in the Banff *Crag and Canyon* on February 11, 1970—well before the disco era.

Editor, *The Crag*, Sir:

I have a very serious problem and feel I must turn to someone.

I am eight years old and am engaged to a very lovely girl, six. I have two brothers, one whom fishes with worms and the other a convict on death row. He killed seven people with a broken whiskey bottle. My mother is a dope pusher at Bassano Elementary school. I also have two sisters, one of whom is an axe murderess while the other dreams up TV commercials.

My problem is this:

Do I tell my fiancée that my father works for the Parks?

The park interpreter insists on a group hug before every guided hike.

The number one scenic attraction is Bubba.

ANNOYING PARKS CANADA

Now why would you *want* to annoy Parks Canada? Don't you realize how much paper work they could drown you in if you got them really upset? Still, it's fun to think about it. I lie awake at night thinking about it. Here's what I've come up with so far:

Slap a paternity suit on Boomer the Beaver.*

When debating park issues, throw around some logic and common sense.

* Boomer—a large, mute beaver with an enormous head—is Parks Canada's mascot.

Return Boomer the Beaver to the wild.

Submit your husband's underwear for an environmental assessment.

Boomer the Beaver—Parks Canada's faithful (as far as we know) mascot.
Larry Halverson/Courtesy Parks Canada

Set your picnic table on fire in an effort to help out with the controlled burn program.

Dress up as a bear and hang out along the Trans-Canada Highway during a long weekend.

Bungee jump off the new wildlife overpass.

Ask a warden if he or she can identify that little grey bird for you.

Refer to the park superintendent as only a "mediocre" intendent.

Phone the public safety wardens and ask to be rescued from the next "Bay Day" sale.

Embark on a career as a serial killer, then apply for a Parks Canada collections permit.

Reserve a group campground for the Hell's Angels next annual general meeting.

TONIGHT'S CAMPFIRE TALK—RATED R

Everyone loves a campfire talk by a park ranger or a naturalist or a park interpreter, or even by some drunk who's stumbled into your camping space—everyone, that is, except the people who don't go.

I think more people would attend campground programs if someone reviewed the talks. For example:

"Two thumbs up, I laughed, I cried, I got my ass chewed off by mosquitoes!"

Park interpreter begins to feel a little horny
before campground program.
Pierre Comty/Courtesy Parks Canada

"Four stars—this is a powerhouse program jammed full of interesting facts, amazing trivia, and the most spectacular car chases ever seen in a campground program."

Campground programs should also be suitably rated for different audiences. The following system may help:

> *General:* suitable for children and crying babies.
> *PG-13:* must have an IQ higher than 13 points.
> *Mature:* no one will dress you up like a beaver.
> *R:* suitable for people who can't tell the difference between a mountain goat and a weasel.

As a seasoned veteran of these programs, I would also like to offer some words of advice on programs to avoid:

Ten Signs That You've Gone to a Bad Campfire Talk

10. Children are asked to cover their eyes during the nude scenes.
9. The fire is used for cult worship and animal sacrifices.
8. Park wardens bust the interpreter for using live animals on stage.
7. The interpreter falls asleep halfway through the program.
6. Audience volunteers have to be rescued by public safety wardens.
5. The slide show features the interpreter's baby pictures.
4. Boomer the Beaver shows up drunk and begins to pick fights with audience members.
3. As the slide trays are changed for the umpteenth time, you notice the sun is rising.
2. The audience is led through the campground in a 250-person-long bunny hop.
1. The interpreter asks the audience if anyone knows when the animals are let out.

DID I REALLY SAY THAT?

Park interpreters occasionally make mistakes, though no one has ever been killed or maimed as a result. Here's a smattering of slip-ups that have taken place in the Rockies.

One young, wide-eyed interpreter continually mentioned the variety of orgasms that could be found in the Rocky Mountains.

While delivering a woodpecker program, an interpreter invited a six-year-old on stage to dress up like a woodpecker. After asking the child where the piece of spongy material should go, the interpreter explained that woodpeckers have a lot of spongy tissue between their brain and their pecker.

While referring to a downy woodpecker, an interpreter assured the audience that the bird makes very good use of its pecker.

More than one park interpreter has made reference to the big, horny sheep visitors might see along the highways.

One poor soul lost a contact lens while removing his sweater. The audience of more than 200 gasped in unison as he frantically tried to catch the tiny, falling disk of plastic. After watching the lens disappear through a crack in the stage floor, a loud "Shit!" was heard throughout the campground. (I forgot I was wearing a microphone.) Down to only one eye, he valiantly finished the program.

While attempting to shoo away a ground squirrel on a hike near Lake Louise, one guide accidentally kicked the poor beast. (Okay, maybe she stepped on it.) Squirrel and audience alike were stunned, but after a few moments the hapless animal managed to shake off the attack and carry on with its business.

An interpreter from Kootenay was delivering a talk to school children on wildlife habitats. To help the children relate to different natural environments, the interpreter explained how people live in different types of homes: some live in apartment buildings, some in mansions, some in duplexes, and so on. At that point a child put up his hand and interrupted, claiming "My Mom says *we* live in dump!"

While changing into historic garb, an interpreter accidentally locked himself out of the theatre and had to knock on the stage door to get one of the 300 audience members to let him in.

One fellow delivering a program at Rampart Creek campground in Banff decided to demonstrate the use of pepper spray (used for discouraging bears from doing . . . well, virtually anything) for the audience. After recounting stories of all the silly fools who have sprayed it into the wind or blasted it into their own face, the interpreter moved away from the crowd and squirted off a generous shot. A few minutes later the first cough broke out. Then another. And another. The wind had shifted. Soon a cloud of bear spray was engulfing the audience. The program was wrapped up before any serious damage was done.

WARDEN HIGHS AND WOES

There's a saying to describe what park wardens do for a living: "Park wardens protect the park from goofballs, and goofballs from themselves."

No, that's not it. How about this: "Park wardens protect themselves from each other."

No, that's not it either. How about, "Park wardens sometimes catch their man," or "park wardens—they love to fly, and it shows." No, that's the Delta Airlines slogan.

Oh well, if I remember it I'll mention it later.

In any case, being a park warden isn't all it's cracked up to be. You have to answer silly questions, bust up rowdy campers, and chase elk out of back yards with hockey sticks—and, judging from the following stories, handle some pretty silly situations from time to time.

The ROAR Files

The ROAR files are "Ridiculous Occurrence Reports," a highly classified set of files that reveal some of the stranger call-outs wardens have received over the years. The following examples certainly qualify for a good ROAR:

Park wardens are called out to help an injured eagle on Banff Avenue. The eagle turns out to be a cowbird picking up litter along the sidewalk.

A visitor reports an astonishing discovery—ancient clay pots found in one of the hot spring pools near Banff. The "ancient clay pots" turn out to be dishes stolen from the Banff Springs Hotel.

A warden gets called out to the Chateau Lake Louise and is excited at the prospect of using his baton for the first time, having just completed a training course on baton use. (No, it's not a cheerleading baton; it's a weapon used for protection in law enforcement.) He got to use it all right—to prod a wayward porcupine out of the Chateau lobby.

Wardens get called out onto a back-country trail to rescue some folks who have been treed by a grizzly bear. The offending culprit turns out to be a hoary marmot.

Wardens receive a report that a steak has been stolen by a black bear in the town of Banff. It was indeed stolen by a bear, off their third-floor apartment balcony!

A warden is called out to remove a bull elk from an underground parking lot. He fires off a cracker shell to scare the animal. It works. Unfortunately, the cracker shot over the elk and scared him toward the hapless warden, who was soon observed by a crowd of onlookers running out of the parking lot at full tilt, with the elk close behind.

Wardens respond to an early morning traffic accident on the Trans Canada Highway west of Lake Louise. One of the vehicles involved in the mishap contains two young women, one of whom is trapped in the car. A warden decides to go in through the car's hatchback to free her. He tosses aside boas, police uniforms, nurse uniforms. He is just moving a blanket out of the way when the still morning air is pierced by a blood-curdling, hold-all-your-calls scream. The perplexed—and shaken—warden soon realizes that he has awakened a large, colourful parrot who had been sleeping comfortably under the blanket. Once the parrot is calmed and the occupants safely on their way to the hospital (there were no serious injuries) two of the wardens compare notes, wondering why neither of the young women appeared to be wearing any underwear. As it turned out, they were strippers looking for work. The uniforms, the boas, and even the parrot, were all part of the act.

Wardens go searching for a couple of lost hikers in the Baker Creek area north of Lake Louise. The couple had become separated and hopelessly confused. When the woman was finally found, the wardens knew without a doubt they had located the right party. She was wearing a baseball cap labelled CONFUSED.

Not Your Lucky Day

A park warden driving down Banff Avenue happened to spot his own dog, Lucky, on the sidewalk. A crowd of onlookers watched as the warden stopped his pickup and manhandled the clearly unwilling border collie into the cab. The altercation between dog and master escalated as the truck continued down the street, the one yelling and pointing his finger, the other barking and growling. The two were still arguing as the truck turned the corner. The warden turned another corner toward home, and found his dog Lucky sitting in his front yard. Oops.

Dog's Best Friend

A warden in the Jasper back country encountered a man and a dog. The man happened to be a friend, the dog perhaps not. The dog was having a field day (literally), running loose and chasing ground squirrels. The warden, of course, had to say something. He told his friend rather bluntly that park regulations regard this as a serious situation, and he had better get his dog on a leash right away. The dog owner paused a moment, apparently deep in thought, then gave the warden an appreciative look. "You're right," he said. "One of those little bones could get caught in my dog's throat."

Horsing Around

Wardens love their horses. They also love practical jokes. Put the two together and you have the never-ending saga of the kidnapped wooden horse. Long ago, so the story goes, the wardens in Jasper had a wooden horse they used to demonstrate horse packing. When a few wardens from Riding Mountain National Park decided to kidnap the beast, the theft was easily accomplished—perhaps too easily. They boxed up the wooden animal and shipped it by rail to Riding Mountain. Another warden who had somehow got wind of the escapade contacted a friend in Edson, Alberta. The friend met the train, managed to retrieve the horse, and proceeded to fill it with manure (sort of a Trojan Horse kind of thing). He then sent the package back on its way.

That started it. After Riding Mountain the horse ended up seeing more of the country than most Canadians dream of. At one point it turned up chained to the Chief Park Warden's desk in Waterton Lakes National Park. Two cunning wardens posing as reporters from Lethbridge managed to convince the Chief Park Warden that it would make a good human interest story. They even talked him into unchaining the horse long enough to pose with it for an outdoor shot—and long enough for an accomplice to steal the horse back again.

The horse has since ended up in regional offices and most parks in western Canada. It was last seen in Yoho National Park. Its current whereabouts remain a mystery.

The Pie-Faced Supe

Wardens from Yoho once decided to arrange a hit on the park superintendent. Pooling their resources, they managed to come up with the $150 needed to procure the services of a qualified assassin. The hit took place at noon while the supe was walking home for lunch. The weapon of choice was a creamy, deep-dish pie with a basement layer of fresh cherries. The assassin scored a direct hit, then fled down the streets of Field, an angry, pie-faced superintendent following at a brisk pace, yelling, "Stop! Stop that man!" The perpetrator escaped in a waiting car, an accomplice behind the wheel, only to be pulled over by the RCMP as they approached the Alberta-BC border. The RCMP officer wasn't told why he was to stop the pair, only that they had been involved in something highly irregular. He escorted the two back to the superintendent. They managed to grovel enough to obtain the latter's forgiveness, but they never betrayed the power behind the scenes. To this day, no one knows who hired them—but a few park wardens have cherry stains on their hands.

Keep Your Ducks In Line

Summer in Banff. The crazy season. A call comes over the park radio: "Duck family lost and confused on Bear Street."

A young woman working her first summer as a park warden arrives on the scene to discover a mother duck with ten ducklings milling about the inset doors of a doctor's office. The ducks are clearly in a jam because the little ones can't fly yet, and a growing crowd of tourists has gathered for a photo op and possibly a little amusement. They are not disappointed.

The warden deftly goes to work. First, she splits the crowd into two rows to give the ducks some breathing space, then (in full uniform, of course) she proceeds to flap her arms, quack, and look as duck-like as possible. It's not a pretty sight, but after a few false starts the ducks

actually buy it. They follow her single-file onto the sidewalk and down the street. But soon they reach a busy intersection. Undaunted, the warden steps into the traffic and stops an oncoming cement truck in its tracks.

She proceeds across the crowded street, flapping and duck-walking, to the vast amusement of everyone but the ducks—and possibly herself. On reaching the far side, the ducklings have to be lifted one at a time up onto the sidewalk, the curb being much too high for their little duck legs.

Gasps of dismay and consternation erupt from the sympathetic but still-expanding crowd of tourists as mother duck, apparently fed-up with the whole charade, suddenly takes flight. For a brief period, warden, ducks, and tourists alike mill around in confusion. Then the ducklings look up at the hapless warden, like recruits awaiting instructions. While they are waiting, the young warden's supervisor drives by, shaking his head in disbelief.

The warden realizes what's happened: she and the ducklings have bonded. When she walks, they walk. When she stops, they stop. When she wiggles, they wiggle. Seizing the opportunity, she turns toward the Bow River, some three blocks away. Squatting once again, she flaps her arms and painstakingly, ducklings in tow, makes her way toward the water. The ten ducklings follow in single file, the tourists in a somewhat less orderly fashion.

The ducklings arrive safely at the water's edge. "What now?" they seem to be asking. The warden is fairly sure she shouldn't start swimming down river. Somewhere a baby starts to cry. The ducklings follow suit. The tension mounts. Then, with a glad honking, mother duck returns, swooping down in a tither to take over from the warden. She (the duck, not the warden) leads her brood into the river and they swim happily away. Mission accomplished, the warden turns proudly and waddles back to the office.

Rescue Me!

Shortly after the "sling-a-warden-beneath-a-helicopter" trick was invented, a warden found himself in a rather precarious position—literally. The fellow didn't have much experience with the harness, and as the helicopter was in a hurry to take off, he just stuffed his limbs into any openings he happened upon. Then he hooked himself to the cable.

When the helicopter took off, the poor warden found he was upside down. He probably had a great view, but the problem then was getting out of the thing at journey's end. As the helicopter hovered low to the ground, the warden reached out and began walking

madly along the terrain on his hands, upside down, in a vain attempt to land gracefully. We'll give him 9.7 for creativity, but only 2 for artistic merit.

> Y̶ou can't really save someone's life, you can only prolong the coming of their death.
>
> – DALE LOEWEN, RETIRED BANFF PARK WARDEN

False Alarm

A light was spotted one night high up on the face of Mt. Cory, near Banff town site. The public safety wardens, being the safety minded bunch they are, decided to investigate in case a climber was in trouble. At first light they raced up with the helicopter, swooping in for a close-up view. Too late, they realized that no one was in peril. The story on the ledge before them, in fact, told the opposite tale. The couple had obviously gone to a great deal of trouble to escape the crowds and find a spot where they were guaranteed a little peace and quiet— and, above all, privacy. (They probably should have put out the "Do Not Disturb" sign.)

SOS

When you're in trouble in the mountains and you don't have a flare, a smoke signal, a radio, a cell phone, or a Collie named Lassie, you have to improvise.

A warden was called out to investigate a possible emergency involving a climber near the town of Banff. He raced to a vantage point where he could assess the situation with his binoculars. Still unable to tell if the climber was in trouble or not, he yelled in as loud a voice as he could muster. He couldn't hear the climber's response, but he needed some indication from the climber as to the status of the situation. He called again:

"Wave if you're in trouble!" Scanning the slopes again with his binoculars, he discovered that the climber was indeed in trouble. He also realized that the climber was female. She had removed her shirt to use as a flag, and was frantically waving it in an attempt to get his attention. It worked.

Another warden had arrived on the scene by now, and asked what was going on.

"Well, there's a woman up there in trouble. I asked her a question and she took her shirt off. She has nothing on underneath."

"Really?" The second warden was not containing his excitement very well. "Quick, ask her *another* question!"

The Horror

Five wardens headed out for a relaxing weekend in the back country of Waterton Lakes National Park. It was typical mid-winter weather in the Rockies: –20°C as the four men and one woman skied to their destination, a cozy cabin that would offer a perfect sanctuary from the bitter cold. Once ensconced in their shelter, tired and well-fed, each of them soon fell into a deep sleep— except for the lone woman, who later compared the ensuing cacophony of snoring to "the sound of a bus making repeated attempts to ram the cabin."

Despite the noise, she, too, eventually nodded off. She was awakened at 2:00 AM by the sound of one of her fellow wardens tiptoeing about the cabin. Call of nature, she thought (there was, of course, no indoor plumbing), and turned over. Half asleep, she listened as whoever it was felt his way to the door. She heard the sound of the doorknob turning, then an unexpected rattling. There was squeaking, more rattling, some heavy breathing, then a good deal more rattling. The door wouldn't budge. It was frozen shut.

It was also the only way out.

And there seemed to be some urgency in the warden's efforts.

Another warden clambered out of his cozy pod and made his way to the door to help. For several minutes the two of them pulled, strained, and grunted in an abortive effort to open the door. The horror was almost palpable as the first warden realized he could wait no longer. He crept—or perhaps he leapt—not quite silently to a darkened corner of the cabin in search of a suitable receptacle. There he realized, too late, that his internal organs were in rebellion. All of them. Yes, he was barking at both ends. His own discomfort was no doubt matched by the consternation of the others as they realized that, like rodents in some giant-yet-quite-well-furnished mousetrap, they were prisoners in their own cabin. As they listened to the sounds of their friend in embarrassed anguish, they knew they were all in this together.

Soon, three adult men in pastel long underwear were crowded around the door trying to escape. They were well equipped for it: one was armed with a machete, another with an axe, while the third wielded a pancake flipper. They were determined to escape or die trying. They did manage to pop the door knob off—a small but significant victory, they thought. Crowding around the tiny hole to peer into the cold, black night, however, they realized there was no way their sick friend could fit through the hole where the door knob had been, no

matter how hard they pushed. So near and yet so far.

They eyed the window across the room. Perhaps escape lay there. Time was of the essence. Their friend was getting sicker. Some things are meant to be shared with friends; this was not one of them. With brute force, warden ingenuity, and a good hammer, the window finally gave way.

As the frigid air rushed in, the afflicted warden rushed out. Clad only in socks and long underwear, the fellow disappeared into the −35ºC night. The other wardens tossed gloves, boots, and assorted protective clothing into the abyss as their friend bounded through the snow to the outhouse. The slamming of the outhouse door brought to a close the terrible episode.

The wardens eventually freed themselves through the door, relieved to see the outside, and even more relieved they did not have to radio for help: "Yes, we're trapped in the cabin. Please send a crowbar, a litre of Pepto Bismal, and a very long straw."

Dispatch Blues

What do you do when you're lost in the 90s? Grab your cellular phone and call for help. That's just what one fellow did, hiking up Mount Rundle. He rang up the Banff dispatch office, described his locale, and asked, "Where am I, and which way do I go?"

Park dispatchers receive many strange calls—such as the Japanese fellow who was certain he had dialled the right number . . . for phone sex. Or the woman who reported her baby carriage had been stolen . . . by an elk (the carriage had ended up draped over the bull's antlers). Or the 3:00 AM call on a cellular from a scared camper: "There's a drunk guy trying to get into our tent."

Cellular phones have changed the nature of incoming calls. Dispatchers now get the equivalent of play-by-play announcers phoning in, giving timely and detailed descriptions of the situation at hand. For example: "The roads are a mess, ice everywhere. Oh-oh, wait, there's someone fish-tailing all over. What an ignoramus, he's headed for the median. Yes, yes . . . ooooohh, that's gotta hurt. He just careened off the median into another car. Oh wait, here's another car, he's spinning, sliding . . . Oh man, he just did a three-sixty spinorama right on the Trans Canada. How about that, folks?" Some of these people are apparently vying for a spot on *Hockey Night in Canada*.

Dispatchers are required to record the nature of each incoming call and provide a succinct description of every incident. The following list, taken from actual incident reports, typifies the range of situations wardens and dispatchers deal with day in and day out:

> Bear now in tent. People in car.
>
> Harassing elk.
>
> Harassing squirrel.
>
> Bear watching exercise class.
>
> Buffalo at large. Headed for Banff Avenue.
>
> Injured magpie. Magpie is terminal.
>
> Elk sitting on sidewalk.
>
> Elk eating up house and keeping everyone awake eating bushes (3:00 AM).
>
> Bull elk blocking entrance to Clock Tower Mall.
>
> Goose in distress.
>
> Someone upset about tree in backyard.
>
> Bear eating at sewage lagoon again.
>
> Elk coming into back door.
>
> Elk with Christmas lights on antlers.
>
> Squirrel in office. Now he's on photocopier.
>
> Elk trapped in ceramics department.
>
> Gopher trap being set up on Lynx (street, that is).
>
> Elk in back yard, attacking toys.
>
> Worried bear on front lawn.

And of course, when you name streets after park animals, you end up with rather confusing reports:

If town planners were to rename Banff streets, they should take an ecological approach to minimize confusion. For example, place the carnivore names at one end of town (perhaps near the more expensive properties); rodent names could be lumped together in areas of multi-unit dwellings; and prey species located near staff housing.

Or we could create a giant ecological web. It would be much easier to give directions to tourists, and driving around Banff would become an ecological learning experience. Wolf would run into Elk, which in turn would contain Liver Fluke Crescent. Lynx Street would meet up with Hare, Marten with Squirrel, and Bear would end up on Cave Avenue. Otter and Beaver would be next to the Bow River, and Bighorn close to Tunnel Mountain Drive. Antelope could be relocated to the prairies, where it belongs, and Gopher would be properly renamed Ground Squirrel Street, and would naturally run into Junk Food Drive. And the steepest road in Banff—Mountain Avenue—would be renamed to start as Elk, but at a certain elevation would merge into Moose (please refer to the silly wildlife questions section to understand the necessity for this).

Coyote last seen on Rabbit.

Elk at Cougar and Fox.

Elk at Squirrel and Rabbit, headed toward Gopher.

Bear treed at Bear and Caribou.

Deer at Lynx and Wolf.

Deer at Deer and Antelope. (Where, presumably, they were playing)

Coyote chasing deer on Badger.

Deer at Wolf and Grizzly.

Injured eagle on Elk.

Bear headed down Moose.

Elk last seen on Deer.

Deer last seen on Elk.

Injured magpie on Beaver.

Distressed duck on Wolverine.

Deer running down Caribou, turning on Bear.

Herd of elk running down Squirrel, headed toward Cougar.

Elk and coyote seen on Marmot, elk headed for Badger, coyote for Cougar.

WILD LIFE AND WILD TIMES

These ground squirrels were busted by park wardens for illegally
camping in a nondesignated campground.
Lynn Widgill/Banff Camera Shop

WHEN DOES AN ELK BECOME A MOOSE?

More strange questions and woolly comments from visitors and friends:

> When do you let the animals out?
>
> When do the elk come downtown?
>
> When do you feed the bears?
>
> At what elevation does an elk become a moose?
>
> What route do the marmots take over Dolomite Pass?

What's the bear situation like on the Columbia Icefield?

Where can I find alpine flamingos?

How do the elk know they're supposed to cross at the elk crossing signs?

Do you see any animals *other* than ice while you're up on the icefield?

Do they ever bring a mountain goat down so that people can see what they look like?

Where do the bears nest?

Can I see your Canadian mammals book please—I saw a bird that I'd like to look up.

Where do I get the animal feed bags?

I saw two black birds driving from Calgary today. What would they be?

> VISITOR: What is the animal that is a cross between a horse and a camel?
> INFORMATION STAFF: Do you mean a female moose?
> VISITOR: No, I definitely know my animals and this is a cross between a horse and a camel.

We saw a moose on the way here—a *live* one, not a dead one.

Are there birds in Canada?

I saw an animal in Banff. Can you please tell me what it was?

Recorded on a wildlife observation card: "My Mom ran over a prairie dog."

> VISITOR: Is that stuffed animal a bear?
> INFORMATION STAFF: No sir, it's a mountain goat.
> VISITOR: That's a pretty one. It looks like my wife when she's all made up. The scraggly one looks like my wife before she's made up.

> VISITOR: How do you pronounce elk?
> INFORMATION STAFF: Elk.
> VISITOR: Oh.

Wildlife watching tip #48: THIS IS TOO DAMNED CLOSE!
Hilary Tarrant/Courtesy Parks Canada

You guys ought to build a garbage dump for the bears.

What are those ugly buggers? (They were bighorn sheep.)

Is it okay to keep an open bag of bacon on the picnic table, or should it be stored in the tent?

Do the bighorn sheep require shepherds?

What kind of monkeys are found in this park?

Could I have a bear idea, please?

Was the mountain goat dead when you stuffed it?

Where can we see a snow goat?

Are the bears with collars tame?

Are the elk with collars pets?

It sure would be great for my kids to see me kill a caribou and butcher it, you know, to show them what it was like in the old days. Is there somewhere I can rent some knives and a rifle?

I have a brother in Kansas who wants to come and hunt your caribou. Where should I tell him to go?

Can I get some hunting regulations for the parks please?

There's a bear warning for Red Deer Lakes today. Can we drive up and take some pictures?

The only wildlife I've been able to see has been behind the steering wheel of an automobile.

Is that a grizzly? (Asked by a visitor in response to the sound of a dog scratching at the staff entrance door.)

Do the mountain goats tan during the summer and turn brown?

How do you get to the Great Bear Hunt?

Do ground squirrels bark?

How many people are eaten by grizzlies each year?

Just how far can a porcupine throw its quills?

Hey Dad, a dog drinking a beer! (Referring to the Parks Canada litter bag picture of a dead coyote with its muzzle stuck in a tin can.)

We went to the buffalo paddock today and were very disappointed when we saw six tired buffalo.

Do you have any of these "What to Do With a Bear" pamphlets?

Where can I get to Bear Country? (Pointing to the *You Are in Bear Country* brochure.)

No, we never went to bear country. (Again, pointing at the *You Are in Bear Country* brochure.)

Are we *still* in bear country?

Has Bigfoot been seen recently in the area?

> VISITOR: Do you talk trout?
> INFORMATION STAFF: No, only English.

No snakes around here? That's cheap, snakes are cool!

Do you have your animals on display somewhere, behind cages?

Do you sell worms here? No? That's a little strange, isn't it?

Is that a grizzly? (Pointing to picture of a hoary marmot.)

Is there anywhere we can see the bears pose?

According to this guide book, moose hormones change in September and they go wacky. Boy, can I relate to that.

Is there a restaurant that serves bear meat in the park?

Where's the watering hole in Jasper where they feed and water the animals?

Do pregnant women emit a special odour that attracts bears?

Do pine martens climb up your pant leg?

When do you have the big animal round up?

Is it true that to escape a bear you have to climb a tree that's the same width as your head?

Don't you groom your animals? They look *terrible*!

Are the animals napping right now?

Can you go whale watching on Maligne Lake in Jasper?

The animals were here the last time we came. What did you do with them?

WATCHING THE WILDLIFE WATCHERS WATCH

When it comes to wildlife watching in the Rockies, size really does matter.
Parks Canada

Wildlife watching is okay if you're into excitement and discovery and adventure and exploring the natural wonders of our amazingly diverse universe. But what's even more fun is watching people watching wildlife. If you watch closely, you can actually tell how long a person has lived in the mountains based on his or her reactions to the wildlife. Sadly, it doesn't take long before locals begin to think of the elk as cows, the bighorns as mere sheep, and the moose as horses. Even the large sexy carnivores (wolves, cougars, Marlon Brando) become mundane over time. The following table should clarify:

Length of residency in the mountains:	Minimum wildlife sighting that will result in sustained attention:
one day	half eaten chipmunk or cow elk
< one month	live chipmunk or cow elk
1 – 6 months	cow elk
6 – 12 months	bull elk
1 – 2 years	bull elk sparring with another bull or elk mating
2 – 6 years	wolf, cougar, or grizzly
6 – 12 years	cougar hauling down a bull moose which has just finished fighting with another bull moose
12 years+	Elvis, a two-headed elk, or a cougar fighting with a wolf pack over the rights to haul down a moose which is fending off a female grizzly with three cubs; one of the cubs is an albino

TODAY'S MYSTERY ANIMAL

Park visitors often approach locals with a description of an animal they wish to have identified. The more witnesses to the alleged animal, the greater the confusion. Any general consensus as to what the animal may actually have looked like is out of the question, and the identity of the creature will invariably remain a mystery.

The following conversation describes an actual

encounter I had with a family camped at Rampart Creek, in the northern part of Banff National Park. It may help to explain why Sasquatch sightings are on the rise:

"Excuse me, sir," said the father of the family. "Can you help us identify an animal we saw yesterday?"

"Why, certainly," I replied. (I'm always so damned helpful. It's embarrassing.)

"We saw it across the river," said the mother, "about fifty feet away, in the bushes."

"It was more like a hundred feet, honey, and it wasn't really in the bushes. We had a pretty good view of it."

"I don't know about that, son," Grandpa put in. "I'd say it was three hundred feet away, at least."

"So, we could agree," I said, "that it was *some* distance away."

"Sure," said Dad. "Anyway, it was big, but not too big. Kind of medium sized."

"Are you kidding, Dad?"—this from the son, or the grandson; anyway, the male representative of the third generation—"It was huge!"

"It *was* rather large, dear," said Mom.

"I thought it was small," the daughter contradicted her. She, it needs hardly be said, was the female representative of the third generation.

"Must have been three hundred, maybe four hundred feet away," said Grandpa.

"Okay," said Dad, giving in, "it was *mediumish* to large, and kind of orangey-brown."

"It was the colour of Bobby's old Buick," said Grandma. "Remember?"

"It had long legs," said Mom.

"Four of them," said the daughter.

"We think it may have had antlers," said Dad, "but we're not sure.

"It seemed like a cross between a porcupine and a deer," Grandpa volunteered. "Could it have been a wolverine?"

"A wolv—" I began.

"It definitely had quills," said the son.

"Yes, quills," said mom. "But it was striped, too. At least, it had one big stripe."

"Do you get wolverines in these parts?" asked Grandpa. He seemed to be developing a theme.

"It was no wolverine"—Dad was definite—"and it certainly wasn't a porcupine. We have lots of those where we come from."

"It was actually quite black," said the daughter.

"What about the quills?" the son put in. "Can we get back to the quills?"

"Well, if it had quills—" I began, again.

"We're not sure it had quills," said Dad. "It may just have had long hair, like a mountain goat, only dark with long legs and a stripe."

"And antlers," Mom reminded him.

"I'm glad it wasn't a grizzly," said Grandma. "You don't think it was a grizzly, do you?"

"It was more moose than anything," said Grandpa, having abandoned his wolverine theory.

"*Moose?*"

"Well, not really," said Dad, "only sort of. Do you know what I mean?"

"No, I don't."

"I'm sure it had antlers," said Mom. "And it was not orangey. It was more gray than anything."

"It had a strange-shaped head," the daughter opined.

"Yeah," the son agreed, "and long claws."

"What about the tail?" asked Mom. "I'm certain it had a big, bushy tail like a coyote."

"That was no coyote," said Grandpa. "I've seen plenty of coyotes, and that was no coyote."

"Are coyotes dangerous?" asked the daughter.

"It was kind of slow moving," said the son.

"Yes," Mom agreed. "And yet, somehow, it moved quickly."

"It kind of hopped," said Grandpa.

"Yes, that's right, it hopped."

"Maybe it was a cross between a moose and a coyote. Is that possible?"

"Don't be a dork. That's not possible. No way."

"Don't call your sister a dork."

"Look," said Grandpa, in the tone of someone who thinks he can clear everything up, "all we know is this: it was large, it was brown, black, or gray, maybe had antlers, maybe not, maybe quills, maybe not, and quite possibly striped."

"So, can you tell us what it was?" asked Dad.

A long pregnant pause ensued, engulfing us like a thick stench. I looked up at the surrounding mountains. A verse from the Bible popped into my head: "I shall lift up mine eyes to the hills, from whence cometh my help." I waited. Help cameth not. Finally, I said, "You know, I don't actually work here."

"Oh," said Dad, "we thought you did."

"Nope."

"So you can't help us?"

I shook my head. "Sorry."

"How come you're wearing a park ranger uniform?" the son demanded.

"I like the feel of polyester."

"Perhaps we should leave," Grandma suggested.

"Sorry I couldn't be more help. You know, I like to be helpful."

"Don't worry about it," said Dad. "We'll find someone who knows what he's talking about."

"Perhaps a wildlife guide book would help," I suggested. (I'd meant to say that family counseling would perhaps be in order, but it came out wrong.)

Minutes later I could still hear them jabbering away about the mystery animal as they ambled down the road. I'm pretty sure I heard the words "penguin" and "marsupial" mentioned in the same sentence.

Attention Wildlife Watchers

If you or anyone you know have made similar sightings in the Canadian Rockies, please let me know. I'm starting a file, just in case there's something out there that actually matches their description.

A HERD OF BEARS, A JAM OF TOURISTS

"Where can I find a herd of bears?" asked the young German woman.

I explained to her that bears don't move in herds. They tend to lead rather solitary lives, and even if they were to congregate in a group we would call it a *sloth* of bears, not a herd.

"A sloth?" she asked. "Why a sloth?"

"Why not?"

"Okay, where can I find a *sloth* of bears?"

For some reason, we humans enjoy coming up with peculiar labels to make things more complicated than they need to be. (This is something of an understatement from someone who used to work for the government.) We could have decided eons ago that *any* gathering of animals was a herd: a herd of sheep, a herd of elk, a herd of bears, a herd of birds, and—yes, why not? —a herd of fish swimming along. But sometime, somewhere, someone decided to complicate things. Fortunately, whoever it was had a sense of humour. He or she decided that nearly every animal on the planet should have a different term describing its particular group. Thus we have pods of whales, schools of fish, and herds of cows. So the next time you're wildlife watching in the Canadian Rockies, use the correct term, or someone is bound to laugh at you.

Your Guide to the Rocky Mountain Herds

A sloth of bears	An army of frogs
A knot of toads	An unkindness of ravens
A flight of hawks	A drove of hares
A cete of badgers	A convocation of eagles
A hover of trout	A whisp of snipes
A siege of herons	A richness of martens
A herd of deer	A gaggle of geese
A pack/route of wolves	A host of sparrows
A charm of hummingbirds	A trip of mountain goats
A gang of elk	A covey of grouse
A murder of crows	A chattering of starlings
A band of jays	A flock of sheep
An earth of foxes	A colony of gulls
A paddling of ducks (swimming)	A flight of swallows
A team of ducks (in flight)	A dray of squirrels
A parliament of owls	A wedge of swans

Parting Thought

It's unfortunate that we don't apply the same terms to human gatherings. We could have a jam of tourists or a confusion of visitors, a ledge of mountain climbers, a waddle of wardens, and a trail of hikers. How about a pad of campers or a saddle of cowboys? I could go on all day. In fact, I have.

YOU ARE IN POTATO CHIP COUNTRY

As long as there are people with too much time and too little brains, park wildlife will continue to be fed by misguided *homo sapiens*. Countless signs and brochures point out the manifold dangers of this, both to the wildlife and to the person trying to feed them. What the brochures and signs fail to mention, because they are trying to be diplomatic, is this: it's really STUPID. However, if you insist on breaking both the law and the intelligence barrier, here is a list of things you should *never, ever* feed the wildlife:

Dear Aunt May: We just love the wildlife here. Right now Dick is feeding our leftovers from breakfast to the

> Flintstones vitamins. (The first law-breakers I ever caught were offering the last of their Flintstones vitamins to bighorn sheep at Lake Minnewanka. Please don't do that again.)
>
> Preparation-H.
>
> Espresso.
>
> Your husband's wiener loaf surprise. (No animal deserves this.)
>
> Pizza. (It gives them nightmares.)
>
> Your brother in-law.
>
> Grape Kool-Aid. (It turns their lips purple and impairs their chances of successfully mating.)
>
> Jaw breakers.
>
> Chewing tobacco.

Any part of your anatomy that gets too close. (It might give a whole new meaning to the phrase "hand-fed.")

JAMMING WITH THE WILDLIFE

Wildlife traffic jams (not herds of animals immobilized by road conditions, you understand, but herds of vehicles apparently immobilized by the presence of animals) are a common occurrence in mountain parks—so common, in fact, that they're the surest thing to watch for if you're looking for wildlife. Forget tracking the animals. Who wants to look at poop all day when all you have to do is watch out for a gaggle of idiotic motorists?

This woman is about to "hand-feed" the bears.
Bill Gibbons/Whyte Museum of the Canadian Rockies/V227-3290

Twelve Steps for a Successful Bear Jam

1. Spouse (male, female, or other) must scream at top of lungs "I see something!" thus causing the driver (who is already preoccupied videotaping the drive while passing a semitrailer) to swerve wildly, narrowly missing a tour bus.

2. Once you have slowed sufficiently, your spouse must calmly state, "Oh, it's just a tree."

3. Continue driving until you see a cluster of vehicles that have already scouted out the wildlife for you. Think of them as your free safari guide. *Now* is the time to stop.

4. Stop the car. Don't worry about pulling off the road, as this will only waste valuable time.

5. Open the car doors. Do not feel compelled to check for oncoming vehicles. Again, time is of the essence. Responsible motorists should be watching for people like you, anyway.

6. Run toward the wildlife at top speed, carrying your camera, binoculars, video camera, and baby, all of which have been strategically strung, hung, or draped on various portions of your anatomy.

7. Approach wildlife as closely as you would the family dog. (Note that at this distance you will have to look through your binoculars backwards in order to view the entire animal.)

8. Ignore comments from park wardens or other visitors who may be suggesting such things as, "You might want to move back a little, sir," or "She's not quite finished eating the previous tourist, sir. You may want to give her a little space," or the always tiresome, "Could you please move? You're blocking our photo."

Wildlife signs were much easier to spot in the early days.
Parks Canada

9. As you have pretty well committed yourself to ignoring park regulations and common sense anyway, you might as well take the time now to share some words of wisdom with your children and the other visitors, who are no doubt ignorant of the fact that "These bears are the biggest marsupials north of Ohio" or "These fellas can rip open a motor home like it was a sardine can. What's that, honey? Are we in danger? Oh, don't be silly!"

10. Watch for subtle clues in the animal's behaviour that may indicate aggression, then ignore them. Such behaviour may include head shaking, growling, raising of the upper lip, or chewing on your lower leg.

11. If the bear *does* charge, you have the following options:
    A) run toward the car, screaming like a wildcat;
    B) throw another visitor into the animal's path (heck, even *Wild Kingdom* spouts off about survival of the fittest);
    C) fight back using your penlight and your son's Batman figurine. You'll look like an idiot, but what other option do you have?

12. Get back into the car and resume driving. Do not feel you must watch out for other motorists as you re-enter the stream of traffic. They have no idea what you've just been through.

SNUBBING GRIZ

There's an interesting phenomenon in the Rocky Mountains: about half the visitors want to know where to go to see a grizzly, while the other half spend their time making sure they don't see a grizzly. The following list is dedicated to those who are seeking definitive answers on how to avoid a grizzly during their next visit to bear country.

Public safety warden Tim Auger has a diabolical idea for avoiding grizzlies. He claims it might be the only foolproof method. The plan is as simple as it is stupid. Simply carry with you at all times a life-sized picture of yourself. When a bear charges, whip out the poster, unfold it in front of you, and allow the bear to charge the likeness of you. Now here's the kicker—the poster is actually created on sticky flypaper which you toss over the hapless bear at the last moment, leaving him wrestling your image, while the real you sneaks off down the trail, giggling away to yourself. Please don't try this at home.

The Best Ways to Avoid Grizzlies

Don't return their phone calls.

Bathe in bear pepper spray before every hike.

Yell out: "Boy, that Gentle Ben sure was gentle." *

Don't use underarm antiperspirant for a week. **

Wear clothes from the disco era.

Hang out in different social circles.

Sing Barry Manilow songs as you walk.

Pretend you didn't hear what they said.

Periodically yell, "I sure do love that Grizzly Adams fellow!"

Staying in your tree for prolonged periods is the best way to avoid grizzlies in bear country.
Parks Canada

* Gentle Ben was an old television series about a pet grizzly. Beware—younger bears may not understand this reference and charge anyway.

** This pretty well keeps everyone away.

Stay in your tree (assuming you have a tree to stay in).

Do the Macarena every few hundred yards along the trail.

Loudly and often, say, "Mmmm, is that bacon I smell over in site C16?"

BEAR IN MIND

Silly bear stories are part of our culture. To qualify as a true Canadian, in fact, you should be required to have had at least one encounter with a silly bear. The following stories show that bears and people have been creating strange music together in the Canadian Rockies for a long time.

B ear stories are like fine wine; they improve with age.

-UNKNOWN

Bear Bites Park Superintendent

The Superintendent of Banff National Park, Tom Heggie, had a rude awakening on Sunday when he discovered his elbow in the mouth of a bear.

Mr. Heggie was having a nap in the yard of his house on Kootenay Avenue at the time. He reports that the bear was a small cinnamon fellow, about the size of a St. Bernard, who appeared more frightened by the encounter than the owner of the elbow.

No real damage was done by the animal. It could be that he was expressing his opinion of the Parks' get-tough policy regarding the feeding of wildlife.

—Banff *Crag and Canyon*, June 29, 1977

Boys Climb Trees With Bear Behind

You never can tell about bears, and that's why four young boys scampered up the handiest tree when a particularly nosey bear interrupted their fort building Tuesday on Tunnel Mountain.

Proper bear etiquette is a must in the Canadian Rockies.
Whyte Museum of the Canadian Rockies/NA-66-415

The four, Jon Whyte and David Fairless of Banff and two companions from Edmonton, were engaged in the construction of a fort when a medium sized bear ambled on the scene. The boys hurriedly took to the trees while the bear first ate the cookies they had brought with them, and then nosed at Jon's shoe. He was wearing it at the time.

Perhaps they hadn't thought of it at the time, but the bear was probably more used to climbing trees than they were.

—Banff *Crag and Canyon*, July 4, 1952

Rumble Seat Red

The House of Commons, which hears reports from cabinet ministers every so often as to their conduct of Canadian affairs, last week learned from resources Minister Alvin Hamilton, that bear's derrieres are being painted red in an effort to cope with what is termed "the bear menace" in Canada's National Parks—mainly Banff and Jasper.

This is the procedure.

When a bear is seen to become too friendly with the tourists, he is captured in the familiar bear barrel. At some time or other during his stay in the contraption he has one of his haunches painted red by means of a long-handled brush, and is then taken for a ride to one of the far reaches of the park and released.

If he comes back to the settled portions of the park, he is captured again and has the OTHER side of his rumble seat decorated. He is once again given a ride into the hills back yonder.

If he is a persistent type and comes back to civilization a third time, he is dispatched to the bear's happy hunting grounds . . .

. . . In the Commons last week, Mr. Hamilton suggested that tourists seeing the red-bedecked bears would do well to take warning and keep clear. Bow River MP Eldon Wooliams suggested tourists be allowed to carry firearms, but failed to find support from Mr. Hamilton.

—Banff *Crag and Canyon*,
July 27, 1960

The following week this ad appeared in the *Crag and Canyon* classifieds:

MALE HELP WANTED

SOBER, industrious man urgently required to paint rear ends of bears.

Must be member of painter's union. Apply Box 25, *Crag and Canyon.*

Man Feeds Bear—Bear Steals Car

A peculiar incident occurred near the Saskatchewan Crossing on the Banff-Jasper Highway on the evening of Sunday, May 23. It would appear that a motorist and his wife stopped at the edge of the road to get a better look at a black bear. The motorist decided to get out of his vehicle, a foolish move at the best of times, and he walked around the back of the car leaving his wife inside it.

The bear, meanwhile, had padded his way stealthily around the passenger side to the front of the car. Having made it around to the driver's side, and espying the open door, the bear decided to investigate the car's interior.

The motorist's wife, seeing the bear's intent, made a hasty exit from her door and evidently frightened the animal or at least confused him for he became agitated in the close confines of the vehicle and inadvertently brushed against the gearshift lever.

The motor was running and the bear's action caused the car to roll off down the road, much to the surprise of the motorist, who had up to this point been wondering where the bear he spotted had gone.

Bears are not

After a test drive, this bruin decides there are already too many animals on the road.
Byron Harmon/Whyte Museum of the Canadian Rockies/NA-71-2880

noted for their driving skill and this one made no effort to control the vehicle. The car did not go far though, before a convenient ditch interposed itself in its path and brought it to a halt. The bear made a speedy exit and the motorist and his wife got their car back, a little the worse for wear.

—Banff *Crag and Canyon*, June 2, 1976

Bear Destined to Wash Windows

Lewis Mumford, game warden at Johnson Canyon, is spending a portion of his spare hours in gentling a young black bear and the taming process has proceeded sufficiently that Bruin will eat food out of his hand. It is rumoured that when the taming is complete, the Park Superintendent will commandeer the bear and either place him in the Cave or teach him to wash windows at the government bath-house.

—Banff *Crag and Canyon*, July 30, 1921

Eau de Ursus

The concept of bear pepper spray is really quite straightforward: Bear meets human. Human does something stupid. Bear charges human. Human whips pepper spray out of holster like a gun fighter. Human blasts spray at bear. Bear is repelled. Bear runs in opposite direction. Human returns to mowing the

lawn. What could go wrong? Well . . .

For starters, there's the dozen-odd reports every year of folks who forgot the old Jim Croce song about not spitting into the wind. Blasting off bear spray into a strong headwind doesn't do anything for your stress levels. You might as well turn the spray into your face and avoid the middle step entirely. Of course, the strange noises and body contortions the human then exhibits are sometimes enough to send the bear in the opposite direction. No animal wants anything to do with a species this confused and silly.

Then there are the legions of hikers who religiously bring the bear spray along, keeping it secure in the bottom of their backpacks under sixty-five pounds of assorted paraphernalia. There are those, too, who don't use the spray for bears but for mosquito control, mouse control, noisy-camper-next-door control, and "I-was-really-mad-at-my-boyfriend" control. The grand prize, though, goes to the campers near Lake Minnewanka in Banff who thought that bear spray works on the same principle as mosquito repellent: they doused themselves in it, hoping to deter any bruins within a hundred miles.

In Your Face!

A young naturalist named Larry Halverson was accompanying a group of wardens on a routine relocation of a mother bear and her cub. Larry's task was to keep the cub treed while the wardens dealt with the mother, and he took his assignment very seriously. He positioned himself beneath the tree and, wielding a large stick, began beating it against the trunk, on the theory that the noise would frighten the cub enough to keep it up there. It worked. In fact, it scared the crap out of it—literally. Larry never knew what hit him. "It was like getting a pie in the face," he said. "Only this was no pie."

"Our Behinds are Bare Because There's a Bear Behind"

A young couple pulled off along the Icefields Parkway to have a picnic. They spread out a blanket, poured some champagne, and . . . well, one thing led to another, and they were soon engaged in the traditional pastime of lovers through the ages (for more details, see page 160). A black

Unfortunately, Larry Halverson has never recovered from the bear-pie-in-the-face episode.
George Sranko/Courtesy Parks Canada

bear happened by, no doubt wondering what the commotion was. The couple, perhaps fearing an unwelcome *ménage-a-bear*, beat a hasty retreat. Not until they reached their car along the highway did they realize that their keys were back with their clothes, which were now likely being consumed by the inquisitive bruin. The couple were eventually rescued by a warden (who are always happy to assist in cases of this nature). He gave the woman the jacket off his back, and they left the scene, leaving the bear behind.

Any Den Vacancies?

A particularly curious black bear wandered up to the Post Hotel in Lake Louise and discovered the automatic sliding doors. The bear, apparently surprised to discover that he was able to open the doors, began to nose his way into the lobby. The decor must have jarred his aesthetic sensibilities, however, for he hastily withdrew from both the hotel and the general area. (Contrary to local rumours, there have been no reports of bears actually booking rooms at the Post Hotel.)

A Yellow Fellow

Somewhere in the Maligne Valley there's a yellow bear. It seems that an enterprising bruin broke into a geologist's camp and, ignoring a sack of apples, headed for a two-gallon drum of yellow paint. When investigators arrived on the scene it was clear that the bear had thrust its snout into the drum, and numerous yellow tracks were seen leaving the site.

Ecumenical Bruins

The 1968 Jasper *Gateway* reported a story of some visiting nuns who toured the local dump to watch the bears feeding. When a mother bear moved toward the group, one of the nuns asked a local if it would attack. "No, Sister, not if you're a Presbyterian," was the response.

What's Cooking?

Locke Marshall began his Parks Canada career at the garbage incinerator in Waterton Lakes National Park. Visitors would frequently drop by in hopes of seeing bears at the dump. One visitor stands out in Locke's mind:

"When do the bears show up?" asked the disappointed man.

"There was a bear here this morning," replied Locke, "but I chased it away."

"Why do you chase them away? Isn't this where you feed the bears?"

"We don't feed them. They're attracted by the scent of the garbage. And we chase them away because it's dangerous for people and not healthy for the bears."

"If you don't feed them, why are you cooking the garbage?"

"I'm not cooking it, I'm burning it."

"But why waste it? Why don't you just feed it to the bears?"

"We've come full circle," Locke thought. He smiled to himself and returned to the work at hand—preparing dinner for the late shift.

Downed and Treed

Two wildlife researchers were tracking a grizzly by air when their plane suddenly lost power, forcing them to make an emergency landing on Highway 40 in Kananaskis Country. That would have been harrowing enough for most people, but these guys managed to land the plane right where their grizzly was hanging out. Having survived the crash, they were immediately chased up a spruce tree. The grizzly eventually left the area, but to play it safe the researchers stayed atop their downed aircraft until help arrived.

Nature's Justice

After stealing some cases of beer from Whistler's Inn in Jasper, a thief decided to elude the RCMP by fleeing through the woods—never a wise choice in the Rockies. Before long he ran into a black bear and was forced to scramble up a tree for safety. This did not deter the bear, who proceeded to climb a tree next to the unfortunate fellow, from which vantage point the animal leaned over and started trying to "whack" the thief out of the tree. The bear eventually tired of the sport, however, and the man walked thirty kilometres to the nearest warden station, where he was promptly arrested.

Silk Pants and Strawberry Patches

A Spanish visitor showed up at the Jasper Information Centre, highly agitated about something that had just happened to him. After a translator was found, the story unfolded. The visitor had decided to take a siesta in the middle of a strawberry patch, *sans* shoes. Looking up, he noticed a bear ambling toward him. Because of the language difficulties, it was unclear at first who shot up a tree. Turns out it was the bear. The visitor backed away, leaving behind his shoes and pack.

Of course, a bear cannot long resist investigating a

pack, and soon shinnied down the tree. Our visitor, observing from a distance, was shocked to see the bear eat his bananas, chew on his shoes, and then devour a pair of silk pants. He thought it odd that the bear seemed to enjoy the silk pants more than anything else. A park warden eventually arrived on the scene and scared the animal away. The visitor was able to get his shoes back, a little the worse for wear, but the pants were a total loss. Perhaps it is a reminder to all of us *not* to wear silk pants while hiking in bear country.

Blasted Dogs!

There's a legendary tale in the Rockies about a black bear that wandered into a construction camp along the Icefields Parkway and dived into the slop hole in search of scraps. As it happened, one of the workers had had enough of bears scrounging about in the garbage, and he decided to make a lasting impression on this one. He grabbed a stick of dynamite with a long fuse from the camp storage shed, lit it, and sent it down the hole after the bear.

Unfortunately, the man's dog, a poodle, had witnessed the whole thing. The poodle dutifully bounded after the stick, emerging triumphantly from the slop hole with the lit stick of dynamite in its jaws. The owner ran for the hills in the opposite direction, imploring his dog *not* to follow. He managed to escape serious damage to his person. The poodle was not so lucky.

FOREPLAY—WHEN GOLFERS AND WILDLIFE MIX

Golfers in the heart of alligator country, Florida, are warned just to leave any golf balls that land in or near the water, or they may lose more than just their balls. In the Rockies, golfers don't have to worry about alligators —just elk, coyotes, black bears, Canada geese, ground squirrels, grizzlies, and the odd raven. A very odd raven.

Elk Paradise

There's a huge salad bar near the confluence of the Bow and Spray Rivers in Banff National Park. It's called the Banff Springs Hotel Golf Course. Wide-open spaces, succulent rolling carpets of green grass, all conveniently located in the middle of some of the best wildlife habitat in the mountains. Imagine an elk wandering through the dark forest and then stumbling upon this oasis. Ah, heaven! It's no wonder elk often outnumber golfers. In fact, when Banff golfers yell "FORE!" they're usually referring to the number of elk blocking their shot.

Besides being the greenest salad bar west of Canmore, the Banff Springs course is also a prime gathering place for elk during the fall mating season, when bull elk gather their harems. A successful bull may maintain and breed with as many as thirty cows (that's *elk* cows, not bovines). This takes a bit of effort, of course, which seems only fair. The bull must serenade the females by bugling (if you've never heard an elk bugle, imagine playing a Michael Jackson record backwards), keep the harem together, and fight off any rival suitors. The fact that strange-looking two-legged creatures in plaid shorts are chasing little white balls through the middle of all this is incidental to the elk, who have other things on their mind. Namely sex, sex, and, well, more sex.

In exchange for green pastures and lots of sex, the elk put up with flying golf balls, voyeurs, and people yelling "FORE!" at them all day. The golfers, on the other hand, get a rare opportunity to commune with nature without ever leaving their carts. They also have the added challenge of having to make shots through the legs of an 800-pound bull elk. Makes the game more exciting, don't you think?

Signs? What Signs?

One golfer was so enamoured of a large bull elk that she constantly approached the animal for close-up photos. The course bartender, cruising in his golf cart, noticed the woman on several occasions and repeatedly warned her to keep her distance. After half a dozen strongly worded warnings, the woman finally went too far. On the fourteenth hole the elk decided he'd had enough of this intrusion into his personal space and charged the woman, sending her scampering back to her cart. This did not deter the woman, who again approached the elk from the (presumed) safety of her cart. The bull charged the cart, knocking the woman off and nearly flipping the cart in the process. The bartender hastened to the woman's aid. The woman was furious.

"How could this have happened?" she demanded. And again, for good measure: "How could this have happened?"

"Are you all right?" asked the bartender. "Are you hurt?"

"I just want to know *how* something like this could happen. Why aren't there any signs anywhere? Why aren't there any posters warning us of the danger?"

"Lady," replied the bartender, "I *was* your sign for the last hour and a half!"

Since this incident, the woman has taken up sky diving, which she feels will be a much safer hobby than golf.

Mission Accomplished

One local golfer recounts a story of being chased by a bull elk one early September morning. He admits his concentration on the game sometimes makes him oblivious to things such as roaming grizzlies, elk, or small nuclear explosions, but he still claims the elk "came out of nowhere."

"It was clear that I had violated his space and he wanted me out of there, so I hopped on my cart and began driving away. He kept running toward me—not full out, just fast enough to keep me moving. Naturally, I was looking over my shoulder the whole time, watching him trot toward me. He kept shaking his head like a wild horse. He was clearly agitated. I sped up, feeling rather silly at this point—a grown man driving a souped up go-cart, trying to flee an angry elk. Suddenly I was given the jolt of my life. Not watching where I was going—one tends to keep one's eye on a charging elk—I had driven the cart directly into a tree. The elk stopped, apparently as shocked as I was. Then, satisfied that his mission was accomplished, he trotted back to his harem. In retrospect, it was a good thing I hit the tree, otherwise I think he would have chased me all the way to Canmore!"

Another Game, Another Birdie

Several years ago there was a raven that took up a rather curious interest in golf, or at least golf balls. After a ball touched down, the bird would swoop in from nowhere and grab it, then fly off, leaving the golfers to sort out the details of how such an event would be scored.

Part of the mystery was solved when a local golfer was hiking on Mt. Rundle: "I stumbled upon this huge, and I mean *huge*, cache of brand-new golf balls, all piled up in the middle of nowhere. This was obviously where the raven was depositing the balls. There were so many balls that I couldn't fit them all into my pack!"

If you're golfing in Banff, scoring a birdie sometimes takes on a whole new meaning.

Shhhhhhh—Please!

Bill Murray's nemesis in the movie *Caddyshack* was a cute, furry little gopher that possessed the strategic planning abilities of an army general. Fortunately, the grounds keepers at the Banff Springs golf course don't have to worry about gophers. They just have Columbian ground squirrels to worry about.

One of these furballs earned a reputation for himself (or herself, it's hard to tell these things) by chirping at golfers on a particular hole. After minutes of silence and intense concentration, just as a golfer was about to release the swing that would deliver a hole-in-one, this ground squirrel would let out the loudest, shrillest

"CHIRP" known to squirrel-kind, thus shattering the moment and causing the golfer to slice the ball wildly into the nearest trees—or so golfers claimed back in the clubhouse as they were forced to defend their pathetic scores.

Golfers swore they would wait sometimes for five minutes, until they were certain the squirrel was either long gone or wasn't going to squeal on them. To no avail. The ground squirrel would always outsmart them.

"It was as if he knew exactly what he was doing," explained one exasperated golfer, "and seemed to enjoy driving us around the bend."

Where's Bill Murray when you really need him?

A True and Honest Report (from our Foreplay History Files)

This is a true and honest report: Hugh Gourlay and Mr. Leslie climbed a tree near the 7th green on the Banff Golf Course on Sunday last, while Dr. Kennedy and Frank Christon took shelter behind the biggest tree trunk they could find. Every one of them got a liberal supply of pine pitch and resin spread on their trouser legs. Hugh is quite indignant—Frank also; Doc just laughed and Leslie is buying a shot gun.

This all happened because a bull elk thought these golf fellows should not be on his run ways, where his herd of wives wanted to graze.

The fellows were quite wise in what they did. The elk bellowed, pawed the ground, shook his head, and told them just what would happen if they did not get off the grass. Fortunately the cows moved away after twenty minutes and the boys came back to earth.

—Banff *Crag and Canyon*, October 9, 1925

TALES OF TAILS IN THE CANADIAN ROCKIES

It's not just the bears that create fun in the Rockies. When virtually *any* wild animal gets in the path of that dangerous, confused, and unpredictable animal known as *homo sapiens boobicus*, nearly anything can happen. And it has. If we are absorbed and confused by the antics of our wild neighbours, I can only imagine what they, at times, must think of us . . .

Only in Banff . . .

A bear is ejected from a Banff store after attempting to charge his purchases.
Whyte Museum of the Canadian Rockies/Moore Family Collection/V439NA66-416

Banff is Canada's most animal conscious town . . . In September 1950, we saw a bear on Bear street, deer on the station platform, and a coyote trotting through the town park beside the Bow River, while magpies were squawking in the trees above him. Black bears, and usually mother bears with one or two hungry cubs, are frequent visitors on Banff streets. They have been known to raid the baker's van of doughnuts, pies and buns while he was within a shop on the main street. One evening we saw an irate citizen brandishing a broom at a deer in his vegetable garden and the animal leaped over his six-foot fence with the greatest of ease—gracefully, in fact. A Banff friend of ours on Buffalo Street gazed out one morning to see a young moose passing the time o' day with his small son.

—from a letter sent to the Banff *Crag and Canyon* from Toronto columnist and enthusiastic Banff visitor Percy Ghent, November 9, 1951

The Cat's Revenge?

Banff may well have a new dog control officer in the form of an elderly cougar who has taken up residence on Tunnel Mountain. At least two dogs in the last week have discovered too late that this is one cat that does not run when barked at. The animal has made no threatening gestures toward humankind, however, and seems to reserve the surly side of his feline nature for that species of canine that delights in chasing game. In this reversal of the traditional cat/dog relationship the hunter becomes the hunted and ultimately the dinner of his quarry.

—Banff *Crag and Canyon*, March 17, 1976

And in 1990, Banff park wardens received reports of a cougar stalking a dog. The dog, at the time of the alleged stalking, was attached to a leash, which was in turn attached to the hand of the dog's owner. Tug of war, anyone?

Squirrel Attacks Man

While government men were having dinner on the banks of the third [Vermilion] lake, one of them was trying to coach a squirrel to share his lunch. All at once, it made a rush and bit him in the leg, then jumped onto another leg and had to be thrown off. Banff is surely making a success as a wild game sanctuary.

—Banff *Crag and Canyon*, September 24, 1937

Stop or I'll Shoot!

A local woman described her first frightening wildlife encounter in the Rockies. No, it wasn't with a bear or an elk, but a porcupine she met in a Yoho parking lot. After spying the large rodent, and believing that porcupines throw their quills, she screamed, made a dash for her car, locked all the doors (you can never be too safe) and rolled up the windows, the whole time cowering below the window in case an errant quill found its way inside. It was only years later that she discovered that porcupines cannot throw their quills, and that she had been in no danger.

Porcupines Again

"I wish the dogs were let loose. I'd rather have them running around than have porcupines running in the back door."

Thus spoke Miss McColl, of Grand View Villa, one day this week. It appears that one of the inmates of the Villa returning home rather late came across two porcupines in one of the corridors, and was so alarmed that he called loudly for help, and was rescued by two of the boys, who drove the intruders out.

—Banff *Crag and Canyon*, September 18, 1909

But It's So Cute!

The drivers of the local livery barns have many a good story to tell of their experiences with "green" tourists. One which we heard lately was of a lady who, after exhausting the usual stock of "fool" questions, insisted on the driver stopping the rig in order to allow her to get out and

Moose who take up smoking are not considered good insurance risks by brokers. *Parks Canada*

stroke a porcupine that was meandering down the road. Fortunately for the nature lover, the "porky" did not wait to be petted.

—Banff *Crag and Canyon*, September 26, 1908

Moose Enters Local Insurance Office—Could Not Get Policy

One of the main attractions that appeal greatly to the Tourist are the deer, and by deer, reference is had to the members of the carius virginianus family or common American deer, not to half-clad members of the human tribe, who daily flaunt the most gosh awful set of limbs to be seen outside of a dime musee.

These small deer roam the streets of Banff all the year through, damaging gardens when the opportunity offers, but providing a fine tourist attraction and no doubt pay handsome, but unknown dividends to the residents of Banff as a whole.

It remained for a yearling moose, however, to put on the stellar show of the season.

Several Banff residents and a few visitors were astounded to see a yearling moose walk out of Mr. Woodworth's Insurance office on Banff Avenue and proceed on its way across the Bow Bridge.

Mr. Woodworth did not sell the moose a policy, perhaps because it was a poor risk, and chiefly because Mr. Woodworth was not present when the moose visited his premises.

The day being somewhat warm, the back and front door of Mr. Woodworth's office were open, Mr. Woodworth having stepped out to transact some business. During his absence, the yearling entered the back door, looked the premises over and made his exit through the front door on to Banff's busy street.

This is the first instance of a moose in its wild state making a business call, but if the Park authorities do not curb this pernicious habit, it will add another chore to the Banff Avenue businessmen's already heavy load and who can foresee but that some day a family of skunks may take a notion to make a few business calls?

—Banff *Crag and Canyon*, August 25, 1944

Wanted: One Ride, Just About Anywhere ...

A few years ago, rangers in Glacier National Park, Montana—I know, Glacier National Park is not in the *Canadian* Rockies, but it's in the Rockies, the story features a Canadian Rockies animal, and it's too darn cute to dismiss—anyway, the rangers were on the lookout for a hitchhiking marmot. Apparently, a hoary marmot had hitched a ride in the engine compartment of a park van and got a lift to the district office. Then he hopped aboard an employee's car and got a ride to her house, where he proceeded to run around the

Marmot attempts to return to his adoptive owner.
Walter Lanz/Courtesy Parks Canada

street until disappearing into a garage, where it remained for several days.

Park rangers finally trapped the nomadic marmot and returned it to the wild, where they attempted to release it. But as the ranger got into his car, the marmot hopped up into the engine compartment once again. The ranger had to forcibly remove the animal, then take off at high speed. In his rear view mirror he could see the marmot giving chase down the road.

Squirrel Eats Volts

So read the headline on January 2, 1986, after a twenty-five-minute power outage in Banff was caused by a squirrel that managed to bridge two wires.

No, I haven't tasted grilled squirrel. That's not even funny.

Hikers Feeling a Little Sheepish

Many a hiker over the years has been treed by bears. A few have even been treed by hoary marmots mistaken for bears. And back in 1991, three hikers near Lake Minnewanka in Banff National Park were treed for more than three hours by a male bighorn sheep. It seems the sheep was a "garbage" bighorn in search of handouts. When the hikers couldn't produce, he got cranky and sent them up the nearest tree.

1-800-Call-of-the-Wild

We've all heard of capturing that "Kodak moment," or seen people trying to become the next Steven Spielberg with camcorder in hand. But what do you do if you don't have a camera and want to share that special moment with someone? It's simple—use your cellular phone—especially if what you want to share is the call of the wild.

Claude Lemieux, a local Banffite, was out one day walking his dog (on a leash, of course) when a coyote suddenly emerged from the trees a close distance away and, much to Claude's delight, began yipping, barking, and howling. Another coyote joined in and soon a full-fledged wildlife symphony was in progress.

Claude thought this coyote chorus was so impressive he just had to share it with his loved one, so he did what any modern day man would do and called up his fiancée on his cellular phone. "Listen to this!" he said, and thrust the phone in the direction of the singing.

A Rocky Mountain moment captured on film when, after weeks of living together, this moose decides to return to the wilds.
George Noble/Whyte Museum of the Canadian Rockies/V469-1536

Once she was convinced that Claude was in no danger, she sat back and enjoyed the midday diversion.

Modest Bull Elk Adorns Antlers With Bathing Suit

On Wednesday afternoon, Miss Betty Lee, of Chicago, a guest at the Banff Springs Hotel, with Les Saunders as guide, was enjoying a horseback ride up the Spray River. Several miles up the trail they met a big bull elk. On his antlers was hung a lady's bathing suit, draped there as though done by the lady owner. The suit was hung from one antler to the other, the shoulder straps holding it in place, quite tightly stretched, and being high up, did not interfere in any way with the vision of the animal.

—Banff *Crag and Canyon*, August 2, 1935

A Bonding Experience

A few years ago, park wardens tranquilized a well-known local black bear known as Kootenay. The bear had already been radio collared, but had managed to stumble into a trap once again. Wardens had no choice but to tranquilize the bear so they could safely release it from the trap.

While the bear was coming out of the effects of the drugs, Gaby, the first wolf in the Bow Valley to be radio collared, showed up out of nowhere and approached to within inches of the immobile bear. Although wolves have been known to kill black bears, Gaby seemed more intent on scoring the bait that had been laid out for Kootenay. The two collared animals regarded each other briefly. We can imagine the wolf thinking, "Bummer. You fell for it too, eh?"

Playing Tourist All in a Day's Work

How do you learn about the aggressive tendencies of the town elk? How do you learn what elk might do when mobbed by photo-hungry tourists? Why, it's simple. Ask a few of your front-line warden staff to pretend to be tourists and approach the elk until you get a reaction. Then, if the animals react aggressively, mark them using paint guns. This was the plan back in 1991 when elk-human conflicts were beginning to escalate in the town of Banff.

The wardens quickly learned that many of the elk don't like having their personal space invaded. As Mike Henderson related, "Some cows not only stood their ground, but would also start doing the Warden Stomp Two-Step. We named the most aggressive cows after ex-girl friends, as their personality traits could be readily paralleled."

In the name of science, the wardens eventually learned just how aggressive elk can be, the tourists probably got some good photo ops, and the elk learned that it's not just the tourists that can be a real pain in the butt.

More People Killed by Meteorites than Buffalo

Many more people have been killed by lightning than have been run over by stampeding buffalo or killed by wounded grizzly bears or by all the other animals of the prairie and mountains put together.

One might also say that more people have been killed by falling meteorites than have been killed by bears and wolves, and yet, from day to day, the newspapers continue to print bear stories, catamount [cougar] stories and wolf stories, and probably they will do so until long after these animals shall have disappeared from the land.

—Banff *Crag and Canyon*, February 11, 1901

The Outcast Moose

"Banff" the big moose, is chumming with the men on the water extension ditch, eating portions of their lunch and drinking from their water pails. It is said other moose have ostracized "Banff" on account of his twenty cents an hour predilection.

—Banff *Crag and Canyon*, November 7, 1914

What Some Folks Will Do For a Little Entertainment

Guide and outfitter Bill Peyto was known for his eccentric behaviour. On one occasion he live-trapped a lynx, tied it to his back, and carried it into the Alberta Hotel bar in the town of Banff. He released the wild cat, then sat back and watched the chaos. After everyone had fled, Bill finished his drink and re-caught the lynx, then placed it in the Banff Zoo, where it remained one of its primary attraction for years.

A Mercenary Ground Squirrel

Wardens were called out to the ground squirrel colony beside the buffalo paddock in Banff, where a rather irate visitor awaited them. The gentleman explained that his car keys had been stolen. The offending thief? A Columbian ground squirrel. It seems the man had been trying to coax the squirrel out of its hole with his dangling keys, when, to the visitor's surprise and chagrin, the squirrel popped up, grabbed the keys, and disappeared into the dark recesses of its home. The keys were never recovered. The squirrel is reportedly

Tourist tries to lure ground squirrel from his lair by dangling a choice set of keys. *Michael Kerr*

wanted in three other provinces on charges of theft, harassment, and public mischief.

Mistaken Identity

A young gentleman was attacked by an owl on the Fenland trail just outside the town of Banff. Owls have been known to attack people from time to time when defending their young, but in this case the wardens think it may have been a case of mistaken identity. The victim had a long red ponytail, which wardens believe the owl may have mistaken for a red squirrel.

Mistaken Identity II: The Sequel

Lake Louisian George Smith was attacked by an owl while skiing at Sunshine Ski Village. George didn't get a clear description of the assailant, and so couldn't say for certain if it was the same owl that attacked the fellow on Fenland Trail. This time, it seems, the owl was interested in the tassel bobbing on the top of George's toque, which it may have mistaken for a mouse or vole.

Deer Dogging Dog

Residents of national park town sites are constantly reminded of the importance of keeping pets leashed at all times. In Jasper, a local dog obviously

A porcupine attempts to improve the view from an outhouse.
Jeff Waugh/Courtesy Parks Canada

forgot the bylaw and, not having his owner properly leashed, began chasing six deer that were milling about the town. He was having good fun playing wolf, when suddenly the deer stopped and turned to face him. The deer, to the owner's astonishment, began chasing the dog, even herding him when he tried to veer to the right or dodge to the left. Both dog and deer escaped the fray without injury, and hopefully the dog will think twice the next time he decides to play lone wolf.

Lunar Eclipse

Some years ago a gentleman went to the outhouse at the Castle Mountain Youth Hostel. Unbeknownst to him, a pine marten—your basic weasel, only bigger—was relaxing in the dark, cool confines of the biffy. As the man sat down, the marten panicked and raced for the rapidly disappearing light in the hole above him (from the weasel's perspective, it must have looked like a lunar eclipse). Unfortunately, sensitive portions of the man's anatomy were directly in the line of escape. The weasel clamped down as only weasels can. There's not much more to say except . . . well . . . OUCH!

Depraved Coyote

Lake Louise wardens responded to a call from a distressed woman claiming she was chased by a coyote while riding her bike near the village. She abandoned her vehicle to reach safe ground, leaving the coyote to dine on her bicycle seat, which it tucked into with gusto. It must have tasted good, because the animal devoured the entire thing, leaving the woman both speechless and seatless.

Skiers Buffaloed

"Are you sure it's a bison?" asked the dispatcher.
"Oh yes, it's a bison," confirmed the ski patroller.
"And it's charging skiers?"
"Yes."

One would think there were enough hazards to downhill skiing without including angry bison among the perils. Sam, a large bull from the Banff Buffalo Paddock, thought otherwise. On one of Sam's regular forays out of the enclosure, he ventured up the Norquay Ski Hill to take in the sights. It wasn't unusual for Sam to escape. He did it regularly, always—and conveniently—returning on his own once he'd had enough of the good life. Usually his escapes didn't cause many problems other than startling the odd motorist along the Bow Valley Parkway. But charging skiers was evidently a new pet project. Fortunately for the skiers, Sam quickly tired of this diversion and returned to his peaceful life back at the paddock.

The Minister Is In

In the fall of 1962, a cow moose reportedly walked down the main street of Hinton, Alberta. The obviously street-savvy moose stopped for a red light at the corner of Main and 4th, waited for it to turn green, then carried on to 9th Street. The moose stopped, apparently turning over in its mind the advisability of turning into the hardware store. Eventually, she decided against it. Locals speculated that the moose was probably looking for the Minister of Lands and Forests, who was in the hardware store at the time of the visit.

The Mosquito Biting Index

A favourite wildlife species of park visitors and locals alike has got to be the loveable little mosquito. The skeeters' aerial acrobatics, soothing music, and feisty personality have ensured the mosquito a special place in our hearts.

Yeah, right.

Since the invention of the wheel, man, woman, and child have all sought new and ingenious ways of eradicating these little brutes from the face of the earth. In Banff National Park, mosquitoes have been sprayed with everything known to humankind, doused with kerosene, and had their larva blown up with dynamite. A tropical fish—the Mosquito Fish—has even been introduced into the Cave and Basin marsh to help munch up the little fiends. The score thus far in the great mosquito battle: Humans: 0, Mosquitoes: 987, 678, 973, 290, 456, 555, 678, 345.

If you can't beat 'em, the saying goes, join 'em. But if you don't want to join 'em (and who does?) find out where they're hanging out. And if you want to find out where they're hanging out, use the Mosquito Biting Index, a little measurement tool developed by the province of Alberta and tested during the summer of 1974. The procedure is simple: extend your bare right forearm at chest length for two minutes and count the number of mosquitoes that land and

According to a 1975 Jasper *Booster* article, young brunettes are the preferred prey of mosquitoes. Paul Sobon, mosquito repellant expert, is quoted as saying, "Mosquitoes will bite almost everyone, but they appear to like brunettes better."

bite you. Repeat this procedure three times at ten-minute intervals and record the average.

Here's the scale:

Bites/Minute	Rating
0	Nil
.01 – .05	Low
.51 – 2	Moderate
2.01 – 5	High
5.01 or more	Extreme

Give it a whirl at your next weenie roast. Just don't let the park wardens catch you (it's illegal to feed the wildlife).

Wardens Sheepish About Prickly Rescue Mission

Park wardens try never to play around with the natural order of things in our national parks—they leave that for the bureaucrats and developers—preferring to take a hands-off, let nature do her thing kind of approach. But when they got wind of a road-side bighorn ram with a face full of porcupine quills, they felt they had to intervene. The ram frequented the roadside and was in continuous view of park visitors. Wardens carefully tranquilized the ram and removed the quills—all fifty-eight of them.

These sheep, abandoned by their mother, have adopted a van as their surrogate mom. *Brian Patton*

Now, bighorn sheep, if they really are the grass-grazing ruminants they profess to be, are not known as munchers of porcupines, so how the quills found their way into the ram's snout remains a mystery. Perhaps he was attempting a back flip (sheep love to show off their mountaineering prowess) and landed on a hapless porky. No? Okay, maybe he just slipped and fell head-first onto it. In any case, the lesson is obvious: even mountain sheep sometimes slip.

ROCKY MOUNTAIN SPEEDSTERS

On an evening stroll along the shore of Lake Louise I had a close encounter of the furry kind. It appeared so fast that, at first glance, I thought I had a UFO (unidentified furry object) on my hands. A closer look revealed the two racing stripes of the golden-mantled ground squirrel.

Now, spotting a furball like a ground squirrel isn't going to sell a lot of tickets on a wildlife safari, but on this particular evening, the unexpected happened, as it so often does, and a common encounter with a most common resident of the Rockies was about to turn into anything *but* common.

Another ground squirrel, which had obviously been lurking in the forest for some time, leapt onto the trail, legs spread-eagled like an Olympic ski jumper. It landed inches behind the first squirrel, James Bond style, ready for action. And on its furry little face it was wearing what could only be described as a crazed look. The chase was on!

Like greyhounds in full flight, the ground squirrels sped down the lakeshore trail. After two, maybe three hundred metres, a cloud of dust filled the air as the lead squirrel spun around in a dramatic 180-degree spin, trying desperately to outmaneuvre its pursuer. The squirrels raced back toward me at full speed. (I'm not really sure what full speed is for a ground squirrel; I can only assume this was it.) Another 180-degree turn. Down the trail. Up the trail. Back and forth. The pursuer was inching closer. Step by step, paw by paw, he gained on the fugitive squirrel. Finally, with a burst of rodentian energy, the pursuer leapt onto the back of its victim. It soon became apparent that this was no mere wrestling match. This, dear readers, was a fight to the finish.

They rolled, head-over-tail, clinging to each other like leeches, tumbling closer and closer to the edge of the icy cold waters of Lake Louise. Suddenly, a splash echoed through the mountains as the rodents disappeared beneath the surface. Finally, one of the squirrels (I'm not sure which; they all look alike to me) dragged its wet body out of the lake and onto the trail. Its hair was soaked and matted, water dripping from its body.

Was this the pursuer, or the fugitive? All I could do was wait. Soon, the crazed look reappeared; this was definitely the pursuer. It began combing the shoreline, obviously making sure it had finished the job. But where was the fugitive? What had become of the intended victim?

There he was! Further down the trail, the fugitive had slunk onto the shore and was lying motionless. It looked dead. Frozen. But constrained trembling betrayed the truth. I could see the little wheels turning in its rodent-brain. It seemed to be thinking, "I'm not here. No one can see me. I'm invisible." The corpse-like squirrel began looking back over its shoulder to see if the coast was clear (even though, technically, we were on shore), then finally made a desperate bolt for freedom. The chase was back on!

This time it turned into a straight-out marathon. No dodging, no deeking, no spin-a-ramas. Just a flat-out, ears-to-the-side, tails-down, first-to-the-finish-wins-all race for life. The two furry speedsters ran almost a kilometre down the trail (which to a ground squirrel is the equivalent of 357 miles).

It appeared the race was over as the pursuer closed to within an inch of the fugitive's tail. But one last dive for the end zone and the ground squirrel disappeared into a dark hole, leaving the crazed chaser in its furry little wake. The chase ended as abruptly as it had started.

What had caused the chase? A fight over territory? Hormones? A bad night's sleep? Who knows? Just one more tale of the unexpected played out in the wild and furry world of the Canadian Rockies.

ARE YOU JUST VISITING?

DON'T YOU PEOPLE FROM CANADA KNOW ANYTHING?

We present the mother of all visitor questions and comments lists, covering touristy type topics we're sometimes not even sure of:

Can I get some information on where to get information?

No, I don't have time for that. I have to see Canada in a day.

Are there any cesspool facilities around?

VISITOR: "No discos, no nightclubs . . . I drove all the way to Lake Louise for a grocery store?"
STAFF: "Well, there are mountains."
VISITOR: "Yeah, but you can't look at the mountains at night."

Do you have a glacier in this visitor centre?

Do they search you at the BC border?

Is the Trans-Canada Highway the rough, bumpy road?

Is there a lake at Lake Louise?

Does the discount on the gondola ride apply to just the trip up, or the trip down, too?

We'd like a room for four people, please. One bed.

Everyone says, "Go see Lake Louise!" But there's nothing here!

Can I stay overnight in the campgrounds?

A hundred and thirty-five kilometres to Radium Hot Springs . . . Is that by car?

So, at Lake Louise, all we do is look at water?

How many kilograms to Jasper?

VISITOR: What does mainly sunny mean?
INFORMATION STAFF: Mainly sunny.
VISITOR: Oh.

INFORMATION STAFF: There was a hold-up on the highway.
NEW YORK VISITOR: Oh, no! You mean someone was robbed!
INFORMATION STAFF: You can go up to the Chateau Lake Louise and have a look.
VISITOR: What's a look?

Is the slide show not working because the glacier damaged it?

Eight kilometres . . . is that in miles? We work on the decibel system.

Don't all Canadians wear raccoon hats? Where can I buy one?

Are there any vacancies in Denmark?

How far can taxis drive legally outside of Banff?

VISITOR: How do you get into this building?
INFORMATION STAFF: You're in it.
VISITOR: Oh.

Besides the CN hotel and the golf course, is there anything to see in Jasper?

How do you convert Centipede to Fahrenheit?

Did you know your highway symbol for a picnic site is the same symbol for a shrine in Japan? (This would explain a few strange sightings.)

Tell me about bungee jumping in Lake Louise.

Any information on Nova Scotia?

Can you help me find a mobile home in Kelowna?

This Whistlers Campground . . . is that a campground?

Is that Lake Louise? (Asks a man pointing at a sewage lagoon.)

Does the hiking sign indicate old man crossing?

VISITOR: Where do we register?
INFORMATION STAFF: For what, sir?
VISITOR: Oh, for anything.

Do we need money to use the pay phone?

Any danger of radiation at the Radium Hot Springs?

So it's 127 kilometres to the Columbia Icefield? How do you know for certain?

Do they have phones in the town of Banff?

I see on your map you have all the viewpoints marked, but can you tell us about the points of interest along the way?

Is there anything to see between here and Jasper besides scenery?

Thank you, that's very Canadian of you.

It's a mile and a half to the snow coach tours? Is that in miles?

LOCAL: Lake Louise is eighty miles from here.
VISITOR: Is that in miles?

Does no vacancy mean they're full?

Do you have anything?

We saw a sign saying watch for photographers. (They were referring to the highway sign indicating surveyors ahead.)

VISITOR: How far to Jasper?
INFORMATION STAFF: In miles or kilometres?
VISITOR: No, along the road.

> INFORMATION STAFF: 104 kilometres.
> VISITOR: How far in miles?

> VISITOR: How far is it to Calgary?
> INFORMATION STAFF: Two and a half hours.
> VISITOR: How far is it tomorrow?
> INFORMATION STAFF: Two and a half hours.
> VISITOR: How far to Jasper?
> INFORMATION STAFF: Today or tomorrow?
> VISITOR: Monday.
> INFORMATION STAFF: Three hours.

Where can I push my wife off?

Where can my husband get really, really lost?

Is it worth driving to Jasper or is it just more of the same?

I was just in the men's washroom and I'm sure the floor was moving. I felt like I was on a boat. Do you know anything about this?

Do people ever come back from that tour?

Is this the place with the question mark?

What does the "?" sign mean? Oh . . . information. I thought it was there because you didn't know what sign to put up.

Does Tunnel Mountain campground have cable TV?

> INFORMATION STAFF: What happened to your finger?
> VISITOR: Oh that . . . I stuck my finger through a bullet hole in our windshield and my friend turned on his windshield wipers.

We are senior citizens and there's NO way we are going to bed at 11:00 if we don't want to! (In response to a campground attendant who had been trying to explain the "no noise after 11:00 PM" policy.)

> INFORMATION STAFF: Do you have an Alberta Accommodation guide?
> VISITOR: Oh no, we're traveling alone.

Your hours say 8–10. You're only open for two hours?

Is Jasper town *in* a mountain or on top of one?

I've got a problem. My car is really full and I didn't realize that I left my child in Sicamous. (There's a happy ending to this story, the child was found—in Kelowna.)

When we enter BC do we have to change our money into the British pound?

Does Paradise Creek look like paradise, or what?

How many miles, and not crazy miles, to Jasper?

Yes, but there's no roads into the backcountry, so how can I get there?

> INFORMATION STAFF: There's a pay phone thirty miles away.
> VISITOR: Oh, how far is that?

Is there anywhere we can go with easy access to serious danger?

No telephones, no TV, but somehow we survived.

Right here, is this the only place?

> INFORMATION STAFF: Can I help you?
> VISITOR: Are you a psychiatrist?

Can you drive in the park at night?

The sign in the parking lots says thirty minutes, so how long can I park there? (Asked by a true New Yorker.)

Does the sign for the gondola say gondola?

Where do I get the ferry? In Vancouver? Oh, that's right, I get mixed up between ice and water.

Can you cut my route out of this topographic map? I won't be needing the rest of the map.

Quick, before we get a divorce, are there any hotel rooms?

Do you have to take the hitch off the car to go up to the lake?

Do you have logical maps here? Is there more than one Lake Louise?

Are the campgrounds around here nasty?

We went to the Lake Louise overflow but didn't see any signs of flooding.*

I saw a sign that says Lake Louise overflowed. Is this true?

Can I use the same money I used in Calgary?

I'll never see you again so I'm going to ask you a dumb question.

I've seen lakes and mountains. Don't you have anything of interest here?

> INFORMATION STAFF: Can I help you?
> VISITOR: We're sort of undecided.
> INFORMATION STAFF: About what?
> VISITOR: We don't know.

So, if I go on this train, I have to go from one place to another?**

Can you help me? My husband's driving me crazy and he won't shut up.

What does stopping mean? Does it mean stopping on the road or pulling over at a viewpoint?

Gondola rides, you say? I thought there would be more Indians and Eskimos here, not Italians!

Is your kilometre the same as our mile?

Where is the Lake Louise dam?

Is Yoho National Park the restaurant down the road?

The elevation is over 5,000 feet? Is that American feet?

Can you get stoned in the park?

Can you tell me a little about the washrooms? (Watch for my next book, *A Guide to the Washrooms of the Canadian Rockies*.)

What time is it in Japan?

---

* The overflow signs refer to a primitive campground (like a drive-in site) used when the main campground is full. It's the campers, not water, that are overflowing.

** Yeah, this is a crazy little custom we Canadians have.

Are there any campgrounds with campers or trailers already set up for us?*

So Banff is an island, then?

Is that two kilometres by foot or by car?

Does anyone here speak American?

> *VISITOR:* Is Canmore elementary school in Banff or Lake Louise?
> *INFORMATION STAFF:* It's in Canmore.
> *VISITOR:* Oh.

What's the difference between going up the mountain by gondola and going up by helicopter?

Where's that small Grand Canyon you have around here?

Are the national parks natural or man-made?

Can I turn around half way down the trail, or do I have to go all the way to the end?

Do you have a pamphlet that shows me how I got here?

Is there a K-mart anywhere?

Is there any scenery around here I could photograph?

Can I ride through the lake on my motorcycle?

$108 for a hotel room? For $108 I want Burt Reynolds in my bed!

Is Jasper a dead end?**

Do the hotels allow you to stay overnight?

I have a map of North America that even includes Canada!

I don't mean any disrespect, but what is it you do here?

I just drove from Lake Louise to Banff town. Where is the national park, anyway?

* Yes. but don't blame me if you get arrested for trespassing.
** Well, now that you mention it ...

Bus drivers at Lake Louise get some fun out of their jobs in addition to wages and tips. One reports on the dear old lady who noticed the pipe that carries the water from the lake to run the hotel generator. She asked: "Is that the Trans-Canada Pipeline?" Another, who was mightily impressed by the sight of "The Canadian" going through the Spiral Tunnels at Field asked: "Does the CPR do this in the winter when there are no tourists to see it?"

—FROM THE BANFF *CRAG AND CANYON*, SEPTEMBER 10, 1958

VISITOR: When will the park be open?
LOCAL: It's always open. You're in the park right now.
VISITOR: No, no, the park, for the kids.
LOCAL: Well, like I said, you're in it.
VISITOR: No, no, the rides, when do the rides open?
LOCAL: There are no rides here. It's not that kind of park.
VISITOR: Do you think I came here to see scenery? I've got kids with me and there'd better be some rides around here somewhere!
(The gentleman canceled his reservations and huffed off somewhere else in search of rides.)

CAMPGROUND ATTENDANT: Are you checking out?
VISITOR: No, I'm from Montreal.

VISITOR: What's the Maligne Lake road like?
INFORMATION STAFF: Good, nothing to worry about.
VISITOR: Do you need chains?
INFORMATION STAFF: No.
VISITOR: Well the sign says "Chains in winter."
INFORMATION STAFF: But it's not winter.
VISITOR: I don't have chains.
INFORMATION STAFF: You don't need them.
VISITOR: Then why does the sign say "Chains required in winter"?
INFORMATION STAFF: Because you might need chains

in winter, but it's not winter.

VISITOR: Oh, but ...

(Finally, another visitor who had been pouring over a map down the counter, turns and yells, "IT'S NOT WINTER!")

Do you accept Canadian Tire money?

Where's the UFO landing site in Jasper?

What is a gorbie? I've heard lots about them.*

Do you know where our friends are getting married?

Is Mount Robson along the Yellow Brick Road?

Can you see Vancouver from the Whistler's Tramway?

Can I have a map of whatever the next providence is around here?

Can you tell me where the Cave and Basement Springs are?

Do you have a list of all the hospitals in Canada?

---

* Gorbie is a Latin term meaning "cute, cuddly visitors from a far-off land." (Okay, for the real explanation see below.)

What *is* a Gorbie?

According to the late historian and author, Jon Whyte, "A gorbie is a slang term used by people from Eastern Canada who have been in Banff for two or three weeks to describe *other* people who have only been here a day or so." The word was apparently coined by the wife of a Lake Louise businessman. When she passed some visitors on the Trans-Canada Highway she thought they looked rather bored, barren, devoid of life, and soulless. So she called them "Gobis" in reference to the large, barren desert of eastern Asia. Somehow the word got corrupted into gorbies, a term rarely used any more, except by goobies and the occasional snookies.

Could you plan my two month bike trip to New York please?

Are there more questions to ask if I think of more?

What question haven't I asked yet?

You people should have tape recorders so you don't have to repeat yourself all day. You could just mouth the words in time to the recorder!

Don't you people from Canada know anything?

ARE YOU LOCAL ENOUGH TO LIVE HERE?

Please check the following chart to see where you best fit.

Tourist	Local
Wonders where he just came from.	Wonders why tourist won't go back there.
Wonders how much mountain weighs.	Wonders how much tourist weighs.
Enjoys seeing wildlife near the highway.	Enjoys seeing wildlife on the tourist.
Likes feeding park wildlife.	Likes park wildlife to feed them.
Wonders what it would be like to live here if they could afford it.	Wonders what it would be like to live here if they could afford it.
Not sure if elk mind being petted.	Lays bet with friends on number of broken bones tourist petting elk is about to receive.
Wonders where the liquor store is.	Lives in storage closet of liquor store.
Enjoys driving motor home.	Wonders who would attach a motor to their house and drive it down a busy highway.
Think it's neat we have so many elk.	Wonders how much money can be made collecting elk droppings.
Needs to ask for directions.	Needs some direction in life.

Local or tourist? You be the judge.
Michael Kerr

Wonders if the wildlife ever eat local pets.

Asks silly yet well-meaning questions, demonstrating a profound lack of knowledge about the local area.

Wonders why Fifi hasn't returned home yet.

Gives silly, sarcastic answers, demonstrating a profound lack of knowledge about the local area.*

THE FRIENDLIEST VISITOR LETTER IN HISTORY

This heartwarming letter was sent to the Banff Tourism Bureau.

> Dear sirs,
> Hi, how are all of you, there at P.O. Box 1298, there in very Beautiful Canada, doing? I sure hope that all of you are doing great, I'm doing great, sirs. Please send me your exciting, wonderful

---

* This sounds snarkier than I intended. Really.

brochure, sirs. Thank-you, sirs. Here's wishing all of you, there at P.O. Box 1298, there in very beautiful Canada, and yours, a very, very wealthy, healthy, prosperous, most wonderful and happiest of brand New Year's in 1996 and 1997, and the very, very, very best of everything, in 1996 and 1997, and always,

Sincerely,
Your friend in Texas,
P. O. Box 533, Amarillo, Texas, 79105-0533

P.S. I *love* you Canadians!

YOUR GUIDE TO THE GUIDES

It is estimated that, at the current rate of guide book production, everyone living in the Canadian Rockies will have penned a book by the year 2001. Don't despair. If you hurry, there are still a few titles desperately looking for homes:

Short Hikes for Short People

Marmots: Fat, Lazy Bastards of the Alpine

Larry, The Loneliest Liver Fluke

Banff on $2,000 a Day

The Tree Hugger's Guide to Removing Sap

The Developer's Guide to Paving Paradise and Putting Up a Parking Lot

Microwave Meals for the Complete Backpacker

Where to Stick Your Park Permit

Siskel and Ebert's Guide to Films Made in the Rockies

The Bears Hump in Waterton

Louseworts and Noxious Weeds of the Rockies

How to Find the Undiscovered Lakes of the Rockies

The Life and Times of Chipmunk Adams

Cross-Dressing in the Rockies

Your Guide to the Hot Springs Algae

The Mosquito: Unsung Hero of the Rockies

The Complete History of Parks Canada Name Changes

The Great Divide: What's So Damned Great About It, Anyway?

A Field Guide to the Field Guides

HAVING A GOOD TIME, WISH YOU WERE HERE

Today, no trip to the mountains is complete without firing off a post card to friends, loved ones, or mortal enemies. The selection of post cards is astonishing, yet there are still some popular images not represented in the post card market.

Post Cards You'll Probably Never See for Sale in the Rocky Mountains

Park wardens relocating a garbage marmot

Close-up of your park permit

King Kong menacing tourists at Universal Studios

Mountains shaped like Elvis

Bear jams

Close-up of the giardia protozoa (the little fellow that causes Beaver fever)

Rudolf Aemmer models for the first "Scenic Outhouse of the Rockies" postcard.
Whyte Museum of the Canadian Rockies/NA-66-1863

Elk droppings

Park wardens confiscating the beer from your campground party

Scenic outhouses of the Rockies

Famous UFO landing sites of the Rockies

Close-up of souvenir price tags

Confusing highway signs of the Rockies

Hot springs algae

Hotel laundry rooms

Highway underpasses of the Rockies

THE COMPLETE BACKPACKER

Heading into the wilds of the Rockies? Here's a checklist of things you'd better make darned sure you pack in with you:

A backpack

Map (preferably of area you'll be in)

Yourself

Windbreaker (should block the wind)

Swiss Army knife (may substitute a Swiss boy scout)

Rain jacket (should be waterproof)

Guide Book to the Mosquitoes

Umbrella (should open and close)

Bear spray (peppermint or menthol)

Toque (makes you look more Canadian)

Bear bells (These don't work; they are generally not loud enough. However, it's fun to annoy the rest of your hiking party with the constant ringing.)

GPS (Global Positioning System, a neat little gadget that let's everyone know two things: first, that you're a bit of a nerd, and second, that you'll definitely be getting lost at some point on this trip.)

Map of the Columbia Mountains (in case you really get lost)

Dancing shoes

Spare change

First aid kit (should include rattlesnake anti-venom)

Camp stove or Wendy's take-out

Inflatable life raft

Sleeping bag or blanky

Yellow Pages (in case you forgot something)

Foamy or air mattress (may substitute inner tube, but not as comfy)

Slinky (it can get boring out there)

Tent (or supply of lumber)

Good reading material (ie, this book)

GORP (or real food)

Twister, the board game (Mazola version)

Water bottle (should fill with water)

Flares

Satellite dish

Laptop computer

Modem link

Credit card

Supply of 3/4-inch nails

Extra pantyhose

NOTE: This list is recommended *only* for anyone heading into downtown Banff. If you are going any further, please check with an information centre or warden office for a complete list.

THE TOP TWENTY THINGS TO SEE, DO, AND SMELL IN THE CANADIAN ROCKIES

There's no time to be bored in the Rockies. When you think you've done it all, try some of the following:

20. Drive your motor home through the Spiral Tunnels.

Some tourists believe in being prepared when they arrive to take on the Rockies. *Brian Patton/Courtesy Parks Canada.*

19. Have a weenie roast at the next controlled burn.

18. Go bobsledding down the Columbia Icefield.

17. Cash your park permit in for some air miles.

16. Go backpacking in the lobby of the Banff Springs Hotel.

15. Grab your binoculars and search for the elusive hairy chested nut-scratcher.

14. Climb a tree, wait for unsuspecting hikers (you won't have to wait long; hikers are always unsuspecting), and tell them you were treed by a cranky park warden.

13. Have a pee along the Great Divide.

12. Hold a "Who's the Stinkiest Camper" contest.

11. Go in search of the stinkiest outhouse in the Rockies.

10. Drop a fishing line in at Radium Hot Springs.

9. Shower at Takakkaw Falls.

8. Get your spouse nominated as a historic site.

7. Identify all twenty-eight species of mosquitoes found in the Canadian Rockies.

6. Find as many Elvis-shaped mountains as you can.

5. Dress up as a soldier and search people at the BC border.

4. Lead a bunny-hop line dance across one of the new wildlife overpasses.

3. Dress up in tacky clothes, then ask a local some really silly questions.*

2. Set up a Kool-Aid stand at the next bear jam.

1. Dress up as Batman and run out of the cave at the Cave and Basin screaming, "Out of my way, damn it — I'm needed at headquarters!"

* Sorry, this has already been done.

ON THE ROCKS

HOW MUCH DOES THAT MOUNTAIN WEIGH?

More quirky questions and curious comments from visitors, this time on the subject of geology and the mountains:

> The mountains are nice, but they sure do block the view.

> When does a mountain become a hill, and a hill become a mountain?

> How high are you?

> How high can you get?

> Is there a bridge across the Great Divide?

> When do the glaciers close down?

> Is that salt on the mountains or ice? It's got to be salt.

> What's the difference between a mountain and a glacier?

> Do I have to use tampons to walk on the glaciers? (Uh, no, that would be crampons.)

>> *Visitor:* What are those things on the glaciers that look like rocks?
>> *Information Staff:* Rocks.
>> *Visitor:* Oh.

> What makes a glacier a glacier and not just a big chunk of ice?

> Who built the natural bridge and when?

> If it takes five hours to climb Mount Athabasca,

wouldn't it be quicker to take a snowmobile?

How long has this glacier been here? Three or four years?

Does the glacier last all summer?

Are those cattle up on the ice?

How much does that glacier weigh?

How much does that mountain weigh?

Is there any park here, or is it all just rock and ice?

Boy, you sure could make a lot of highballs with that chunk of ice!

Those glaciers don't have as much glace on them as I thought they would.

Does the United States still own this mountain?

Which one of the glaciers started advancing after the California earthquake?

Do the glaciers explode?

Does the "Bumps Ahead" sign refer to mountains?

Are these the only glaciers in the world?

These mountains are pretty mental, eh?

Are there any glaciers in Glacier National Park?

Is there a refreshment stand at the top of Castle Mountain?

I understand the earth is molten inside.

Is there a volcano you can look down inside around here?

Are the mountains lit up at night with flood lights so we can see them?

Can we ride our motorcycles to the top of a mountain somewhere? We don't want to walk anywhere.

> *VISITOR:* I'd like to see the glacier moving, do I have enough time?
> *LOCAL:* Sure, if you have a couple of decades to spare.

Hey mister, if you stick your finger in this spring and plug it up, will the mountain blow up? (Asked by a small child while on a guided tour of Maligne Canyon in Jasper)

Are the rocks in the river natural or does Parks Canada put them there?

The Columbia Icefield: Land of Confusion

The Columbia Icefield deserves a special prize for the most number of strange and wonderful questions. Regardless of where the questions were collected, locals always seem to have a silly Columbia Icefield question on hand.

Is it better to take the snow coach when it's sunny or raining?

Do they rent ice boats here?

Where is the armoured car tour onto the ice?

Where can I go for a horseback ride on the icefield?

Do you have a picture of these Ice Capades?

When do the Ice Capades start?

Can I ride the tractor onto the ice?

I guess there's nothing to see on the snow coach tours, eh? No flowers or anything?

Visitors tour the Columbia Icefield in an early model motorhome.
Bill Gibbons/Whyte Museum of the Canadian Rockies/V227-4173

How long is the forty-five-minute snow coach tour?

Is the snow coach road also the road to Terrace, BC?

Can you tell me where this big thing is? (The "big thing" was the Columbia Icefield.)

So it's just ice? You just go and look at it, or what?

Is this the world's only drive-in glacier?

It's a shame, all that ice going to waste.

Does the Athabasca glacier want to go, or is it just gravity?

Does the Columbia Icefield end in Alaska?

Twenty-five years ago I went up onto the ice in a little weasel.

Oh—*that's* the glacier there? It just looks like a big bunch of snow. (A visitor's remark after spending two days in the area.)

Are the ice walks strenuous? I mean, can wives do them?

Where do we catch the moon buggy?

What's the time difference between the three-hour ice walk and the five-hour ice walk?

With these crisp mornings and hot days, the Columbia Icefield is just like where I come from— Hawaii!

Where do I get the snowboat trip?

Oh sure, if they use ice shoes and pickles they can walk out onto the ice.

Is this the Snow Cow tours?

Can I drive my 4 x 4 on the Columbia Icefield?

Can I snowboard on the Columbia Icefield?

Can kids slide down the ice?

I'd like to go for a ride over all those icicles.

Will the ice already be there when we get to the Columbia Icefield?

Is this the Ricefields?

Where are the boat trips at the Columbia Icefield?

Can I go to the icefield any time? I'm heading up to the Arctic Circle today.

Are the tar sands at the Columbia Icefield?

When does the ice move out at the Columbia Icefield?

If we just stay on the snow coach tour, will we end up in Jasper?

So, what's the big deal with the Columbia Icefield, anyway?

> *VISITOR:* The road on the snow coach tour, is it steep going up?
> *INFORMATION STAFF:* Yes.
> *VISITOR:* How about going back down?

From the "Hope They Were Joking" File

Received on a Visitor Comment Form at the Columbia Icefields Centre: "To eradicate the problem of people parking in designated bus only areas, might I suggest issuing drivers small caliber handguns to first, fire a warning shot over the head of the offender, and secondly, if that should fail, randomly chose one or two offenders per day to set an example and shoot them."

In a letter sent to the Banff National Park superintendent's office: "These rocks were improperly removed from the Columbia Icefield area, please return them to their proper place."

And to add to the suspicion that strange things do indeed happen in the Columbia Icefield area, this quote from the Jasper *Booster* in 1970: "We heard a rumour of some hush-hush goings on at the Icefield involving some equipment for use on the moon. We knew the terrain in the park was varied but this is carrying things a little far."

GEOLOGY MADE SIMPLE

To really understand the Rockies, one must become familiar with some basic geological terminology. These terms, however, can be confusing. Not to worry, I'm here to help.

Alluvial fan: a person who *really* likes alluvials, sometimes to the point of obsession.

Crevasse: the crack exposed on the side of a mountain when a climber's tights don't quite fit.

Erratic: the driving pattern of a tourist who is attempting to videotape the trip while simultaneously changing the baby's diapers.

Frost heaving: what happens after you've had one too many milkshakes.

Glacial advance: what an icefield sometimes does at parties after its had too much to drink.

Hanging glacier: when someone's underwear hangs out of his pants after a foray to the washroom, as in, "Hey, Joe, looks like you've got a bit of a hanging glacier happening."

Hot springs ecology: the science that involves the study of ecosystems that have been severely altered by human sweat, pee, and . . . well, other bodily fluids we don't want to get into.

Icefield: a Canadian term for an outdoor hockey rink.

Igneous intrusion: when a guy named "Igneous" tries to muscle in on your camping trip.

Little Ice Age: a period six summers ago when unusually cool temperatures for three consecutive days caused meteorologists to panic.

Rocky Mountain trench: a term used to describe a pothole in mountain highways.

Scree: the noise a pika makes when you step on it.

Terminal moraine: a moraine that has only a short time to live.

Trilobites: a condition similar to the "trots" experienced by visitors with a minor case of giardia (beaver fever), as in, "Poor Ted, he's got a bad case of the trilobites."

Tufa: a food substitute when even tofu isn't available.

A TRIBUTE TO THE LITTLE BUBNOFF

As we have seen in some of our silly visitor questions, our American friends tend to get a little confused by the metric system. Thank God they haven't met the Bubnoff. As Ben Gadd, author of *Handbook of the Canadian Rockies*, says, "the Bubnoff should be nominated for the 'Funniest-Sounding Unit of Measure'." I agree—and, since I agree, that makes two of us, certainly enough to make it official.

Try using "Bubnoff" in a sentence: "Honey, how's your Bubnoff feeling? Has the swelling come down yet?" Or: "Hey, Larry, let's grab a couple of Bubnoffs after work." Or how about: "Wow, did you see the way the frisbee bubnoffed off his head?"

The Bubnoff, in fact, is a geological unit which represents one millimetre of land-surface reduction per thousand years. The unit can be used to estimate the amount of material that is being eroded and carried away in rivers. At current rates of erosion ("Bubnoffage," as I love to say), Ben Gadd has estimated that Mt. Robson, the highest mountain in the Canadian Rockies, will be as flat as Edmonton in 54,766,656 years and a couple of months—give or take a few Bubnoffs.

ELVIS HAS LEFT THE PARK

Mountains come in an astonishing array of shapes and sizes. Castle Mountain looks like a castle (go figure). The Mitre near Lake Louise looks like a bishop's hat, and Mount Molar looks like—you guessed it—someone's back tooth. If you look at the top of Mt. Hector, north of Lake Louise, you can see Snoopy lying on his back, and on Mt. St. Nicholas you can spy jolly old St. Nick. Nearly every mountain looks like someone or something. You can daydream your life away imagining the faces of different people in our mountains. Look

The king of rock is a prominent, albeit elusive, figure in the Canadian Rockies. *Parks Canada*

over there—it's Prince Charles! And up there—it's Bullwinkle. And wait . . . over there, it looks like . . . yes, it's definitely Bob Hope!

Can you see how this might be fun?

The face most often seen in our mountains belongs to Elvis.* "Elvis, Elvis, Elvis." You hear his name on the lips of visitors straining their necks to peer up at our towering peaks. Often, motorists along the Icefields Parkway will create what's known locally as an Elvis jam as they congregate around the base of yet another Elvis-lookalike pinnacle. So in honour of the king of rock, here's the most up-to-date list of mountains that look like Elvis. I've tried to be as thorough as possible. Please accept my apologies if I've missed any.

> Mt. Indefatigable
>
> Sunwapta Peak
>
> Mt. Kindersley
>
> The Three Sisters (Look closely at the middle sister.)

---

* I have no proof of this. But once I've written this piece I'll be able to refer to it as the definitive source.

Mt. Lefroy

Mt. Edith Cavell (Only when viewed from the south-east, late in the day, from early September till late October.)

Mt. Wardle

Mt. Fernie

Cascade Mountain

Pyramid Mountain

Mt. Yamnuska

Mt. Wilson (Some claim this mountain actually bears a closer resemblance to Buddy Holly.)

Mt. Blakiston

Cathedral Mountain

Mt. Bourgeau

CLIMBING THE WALLS

Mountain climbers spend considerable time at high elevations. It is only to be expected that some of them will have gone a little wonky from the effects of the altitude. Certainly, ample evidence of this is seen in the names they've given to some of the routes they climb. There are hundreds of sport climbs in the Rockies, but only three of those have normal names, so our judges had a difficult time selecting the wackiest ones. The guidelines were simple: anything that made us smile, laugh, or go "Huh?" was chosen. Here, then, is a compendium of the weirdest sport climbing route names found in the Canadian Rockies:

Attack of the Killer Tomatoes	Winnebago Warrior
All Chalk, No Action	Bandits at Two O'clock
Big Crack Attack	Bob's Yer Uncle
Bunny Duck Roof	Bozoids From Plant X
Color Me Psycho	Burnt Weenie Sandwich
Digital Destruction	Cafe Rambo

Duck of Death

The Eggplant that Ate Chicago

The Eggplant's Revenge

Escape from Nap Town

Flesheater

Freaky Styley

Goofy's Gamble

I Wanna Be a Cowboy

Lap Happy

Lube Job

Lunatic Fringe

Men Without Shadows

Moe and Larry Go to France

Nuts of Steel

One Hour Martinizing

One Way to Wangland

Playing With Myself

Poodle on a Leash

Poplar Mechanics

Ravin' Raven

Reclining Porcupine

Repining Porcuclimb

Return of Eggplant

Scary Monsters

The Scorn of Bullwinkle

Sisyphus Goes to Hollywood

Snorting Drano

Something Nice for Sweet Pea

Cerebral Goretex

Chips are for Kids

The Devil Drives

Dr. Tongue's 3-D House of Beef

Excitable Boy

Gravity Rodeo

Grime and Punishment

Hockey Night in Canada

Is That Your Dog?

It's Not the Length That Counts

Junior Woodchuck Jamboree

Lunch Rambo Style

Dr. Risk Goes to Hollywood

Schlomo's Nose Job

Mona Lisa Overdrive

This Bolt's for You

Necrophilia and Fatboy

Lotus Crack

Nestor Overdrive

Monkey in a Rage

Moonabago

Octopoids from the Deep

Penguin Lust

Squirrel Breath

Teddy Bear's Picnic

Tintin and Snowy Get Psyched

Watusi Wedding

Astro Warden

Son of Eggplant

Sounds Like Sex

Square Root of Purple

Squid Crack

Static Fanatic

Superior Cackling Chickens

Toledo Milkmaid

Umma Gumma

Up the Down Staircase

Wild Turkey Surprise

Vulcan Princess

Midgets Mantle

The Duck of Death

Sheep Thrills

Chocolate Bunnies from Hell

Swordfish Trombone

Mr. Rodgers Smokes a Fat One

Monkeylust

Tricks With Mirrors (aka Beats Me Up)

Where Heathens Rage

Big Breasted Girls Go to the Beach and Take Their Tops Off

The Wackiest Waterfall Climbing Routes

The best time to climb waterfalls, of course, is when they're frozen. (Just thought I'd clear that up.) Here are the wackiest waterfall climbing route names in the Canadian Rockies:

Acid Howl

Malignant Mushroom

Nightmare on Elm Street

Bored for November

Pitches of Eastwick

Popsicle Toes

Burning in Water, Drowning by Flame

Scotch on the Rocks

Ceramic Engineer

Shining Nobodies

Drip at the Centre of the Universe

Tales of Ordinary Madness

Knuckle Gnasher

Weathering Heights

I Scream

Elderly Man's Day Out

Grecian Formula

Dr. Heckle

Lizard Lips

Ingredient Sixteen

Malignant Mushroom

Nothing But the Breast

Silver Tongue Devil

Lovely Parting Gifts

Whoa, Capitaine!

Popsicle Stand

Private Functions

The Brains Behind the Names

What twisted minds lurk behind these route names? To find out, I sat down with Mark Whelan, a local climber from Canmore, Alberta. Mark struck me as your typical climber—easygoing, full of energy, and a little warped.

"So Mark," I said, "what's up with these wacky route names?"

"I don't know," he replied, adding, "They're pretty wacky, aren't they?"

"Yup."

After a long silence, I decided to carry on with the interview.

"So Mark," I said, "what are some of the goofier names you've christened routes with yourself?"

"Well, let me see, " he said. "*Superior Cackling Chicken*, *Unforgiven*, and *Duck of Death* are all mine."

"Do you have a personal favourite?"

"*Teddy Bear's Picnic* is one of my favourites. I named it after climbing up a section of wall named *Picnic Lunch*. The climb seemed kind of easy and laid back, so I thought *Teddy Bear's Picnic* would give it a warm, fuzzy feeling and fit into the *motif* of the larger wall."

"Do you ever want to climb a route just because of its name?"

"*Burning in Water and Drowning in Flame* is one I'd like to climb just because of it's name. *The Nose* is another one that inspires me. I like a lot of the French names, too; *Toboggan de la Mort* has a nice ring to it."

"What's your inspiration for coming up with these names?" I asked him. "Drugs? Oxygen deprivation?"

"I get inspiration from a number of different sources," he replied. "I keep a file of potential route names. I've got close to 150 on hand right now. I get the ideas from everywhere. A lot of them I get from CBC radio. Others I get from children's books, movies, songs, or music groups. I think *Bare Naked Ladies* is an ideal name for a route, or the jazz musician Manu Dbangou. I like the way that rolls off the tongue."

"Do you try to match a name to a particular route?"

"Sometimes it will be a name that could have been given to any number of routes. Ideally, though, the name reflects something about the route, or perhaps your mood on that particular day. I think the best names say something about the nature of the route or your first climb on it. In some ways, the name is your personal signature, your stamp on the route."

"What, then, does *Superior Cackling Chickens* have to say about your mood on that particular day?"

"That one I came up with for two reasons: I'd eaten an egg sandwich that day, and I was a bit nervous on the climb, so I guess cackling chickens just popped into my head."

"Is there competition among climbers to come up with weirder and weirder names?"

"There are more and more routes being worked out all the time," he explained, "so coming up with an original name that actually says something about the route can be as competitive as doing the climb itself."

"Do you think climbers in general have a good sense of humour?" I asked. "If so, why?"

"I think climbers do have a good sense of humour— maybe a somewhat warped sense of humour. Perhaps it's part of the lifestyle, living on the edge. They definitely are a distinctive bunch. The climbers who come up with some of these names are obviously very creative. I think you have to be creative to climb successfully. For me, completing a new route is in some ways like painting a picture."

"That's deep."

"Yes."

Unsure of how to end the interview, I asked Mark again what was up with those wacky route names: "So

Mark, like, what's up with those wacky route names?"

"Weren't you listening?"

"Yeah, well . . . thanks for the insights, Mark. May all your future climbs be wacky."

"It's not the climbs that are wacky," he objected, "it's the names."

"I've been trying to think up some names myself," I told him. "Tell me what you think of this: *Rigor Mortis Set in After the Meatloaf Sandwich from Toledo Ate My Sister*."

"Uh, look at the time. I really have to go."

"I take that as a 'no comment.'"

"Yup."

A HYSTERICAL HISTORY OF THE ROCKIES

THE FIRST SILLY VISITOR QUESTIONS AND COMMENTS

Someone, some time, had to have been the first person to ask a really silly question in the Rockies. Maybe it sounded like this:

> Do these mountains go all the way to the Pacific Ocean? I've got to get to China fast.

> That mountain over there: I know no one's climbed it or even named it yet, but can you tell me how much it weighs?

> Hey, Mr. Rogers, do you think this is a good place for the railway? The passengers will have a great view of the Kicking Horse River!

> So, how's the fishing at the Lake of Little Fishes?

> If we set aside a park here, Mr. Prime Minister, do you think anyone will actually come?

> Who would be stupid enough to pay good money to soak in these hot springs?

> There's hardly any elk here now. If we bring in more, they'll never survive.*

---

* A herd of sixty-three Yellowstone elk was relocated to Banff in 1917 to supplement the low population in the park at the time. Elk heaven was awaiting them. Much of the park had been burned and most predators eliminated, setting the stage for a baby boom and contributing to the creation of the present-day urban elk subspecies—*cervus elaphus urbanus*.

Where did I just come from?

Hey, is this zoo the only place you have the animals in cages for us to see?*

What do you mean, it's going to take me three weeks to get to Jasper? What do you mean, there's no road yet?

You mean, I came all the way to Jasper and all I got was this lousy T-shirt?

Who's going to care if we build a town in the middle of this god-forsaken wilderness?

Besides the zoo, the dumps, and the roads, are there any other good places to feed the bears?

HUMOUR IN THE ROCKIES:
THE EARLY YEARS

The Rocky Mountains have a long and colourful history, even though most historic photos are in black and white. In fact, some of the oldest archaeological sites in Canada (dating back more than 11,000 years) have been found near the Vermilion Lakes and Lake Minnewanka in Banff National Park.

Often these early "visitors" are referred to as the early people. Why were they early? Simple: they had no watches, no clocks, no accurate means of telling the time other than the position of the sun. Without the accuracy of modern timepieces, they were always showing up early for things.

Native people played an important role in the history of the mountains. They knew the landscape intimately and led many of the first white people to the lakes and mountain tops, acting as guides to these (in some cases) very lost souls. Undoubtedly, they had to

---

* There was a zoo in Banff town site from 1904 to 1937, located on the grounds of the Park Museum. More than sixty animals were kept there, including monkeys and a rather famous polar bear known as Pat. The odd visitor still asks about the zoo.

put up with the first silly visitor questions:

> What do you think, could we build a railway through here?
>
> Do you mind if we move in for a while?"

There is ample evidence that humour was prevalent among these early natives. One example is the whoopee cushion and Groucho Marx eye glasses found among the remains of a campsite dating back nearly 8,000 years.* A reminder, perhaps, of happier times in these ancient mountains.

A CHRONOLOGY OF ROCKY MOUNTAIN HUMOUR

700 BC — Early natives camping along the shore of Lake Minnewanka bury strange objects as a joke on future archaeologists.

600 BC – 1800 AD Long period with very dry humour.

1807 — While travelling to Howse Pass, explorer and fur trader David Thompson asks his native guide how much Mt. Wilson weighs. Two Stoney Indians are later heard referring to Thompson as a "gorbie."

1858 — James Hector of the Palliser Expedition is the first known white person to get truly lost and ask a native where he just came from.

1878 — Sir Sanford Fleming suggests that a railway could easily be built through the Rockies, but only if they go through the Kicking Horse Canyon. Years later, this is revealed to have been a joke: "I never thought they'd actually do it!"

1883 — Three young railway workers are the first to break in after hours and go skinny dipping at the Cave and Basin hot springs.

---

* Some archaeologists maintain that an error was made in the dating of this particular site, and that, in fact, the site dates back only to last summer, probably early July.

A man either in love with his horse or desperately
missing his sheep.
Whyte Museum of the Canadian Rockies/NA-66-1913

Not everyone is up to trail riding in the Rockies.
Byron Harmon/Whyte Museum of the Canadian Rockies/NA-71/6006

"I've told you men a thousand times—don't feed the chipmunks!"
Whyte Museum of the Canadian Rockies/NA-66-1656

A typical rush hour in the Canadian Rockies.
George Noble/Whyte Museum of the Canadian Rockies/V469-1185

After labour day weekend, the pace in Banff tends to slow down a bit.
A.B. Thom/Whyte Museum of the Canadian Rockies/NA-66-1796

A survivor of the *Titanic* somehow finds herself
adrift in Lake Louise.
*Frank Freeborn/Whyte Museum of the Canadian
Rockies/NA-66-1926*

1885	A national park reserve is created around Sulphur Mountain, laying the groundwork for years of future humour initiated (though unintended) by Parks Canada.
1888	CPR General Manager Van Horne discovers the nearly completed Banff Springs Hotel has been built backwards as a practical joke on future guests.
1894	A mountaineer near Lake Louise asks if his first ascent will only count going up.
1904	The first automobile enters Banff Park along the railway tracks and creates the only bear jam on record in which the bears actually outnumbered the cars.
1905	Alberta becomes a province, setting the wheels in motion that will eventually see a provincial premier named "Ralph."
1909	Legendary guide and eccentric Bill Peyto releases a live lynx in a Banff bar.
1911	A confused visitor in Jasper asks, "Is this the end?"
1925	Mt. Alberta, one of the most difficult ascents in the Rockies, is first climbed by a party of Japanese. Having

An important historical footnote in the Rockies was the development of the first battery-operated pack horse.
Elliot Barnes/Whyte Museum of the Canadian Rockies/NG-9-60

embarrassed the Canadians, the Japanese decide to lay low in the town of Banff for a few years.

1930   The National Parks Act is passed, ensuring that "sex in the outdoors" is a legitimate and appropriate activity within national park boundaries.

1954   Marilyn Monroe and Robert Mitchum are swept over the Bow Falls, Hollywood-style, for the movie *River of No Return*. Marilyn's hair never looked better.

1962   The Trans-Canada Highway is opened with great fanfare. A politician is overheard saying, "It's a good thing we have these national parks or we'd have nowhere to put this highway!"

1996   The Banff Bow Valley Study is released. (It seems to have been released somewhere in the remote back country of Banff National Park. If anyone finds it, please notify the nearest Missing Studies office.)

1997   After survey results regarding Parks Canada's beaver logo is released, a Calgary radio station phones the Minister of Canadian Heritage in hopes of asking her if her beaver looks like a pork chop. The Minister is not amused.

1998   This book is published, upsetting historians over "gross historical inaccuracies."

DON'T QUOTE ME

History is full of great people who made intelligent and insightful observations. And then there are these folks, from the journals of yesteryear in the Canadian Rockies:

> It is doubtful whether any five men went into a pathless wilderness knowing less than we did of the supremely important subject of camp cooking.
>
> —Yandell Henderson, 1893,
> describing his Yale mountaineering team

> The instant my eyes rested on the broad shining surface of its buffer beam and cowcatcher . . . I decided to travel there and nowhere else for the remaining 600 miles of my journey.
>
> —Lady Agnes, wife of Prime Minister
> John A. Macdonald, moments before climbing
> aboard the cowcatcher of her train in 1887

> An hour more and we began to get views; views so wonderful so as to make even the ladies forget their fluttering skirts and clogging petticoats and fast disintegrating boots.
>
> —Ralph Connor, 1907,
> describing a climb up Cascade Mountain

> It takes us a full week, the greater part of it spent in bed, to realize that mountaineering climbing *sans* guides, *sans* mountaineering boots, *plus* petticoats, is a pastime for angels perhaps, but not for fools.
>
> —Ralph Connor, again

> I hope I won't lose them, Doctor, I've had 'em a long time and I'm sort of used to 'em.
>
> —Tom Wilson, guide and outfitter,
> talking to his doctor about his frost-bitten feet
> after a seventy-mile snowshoe trip over the mountains to eat Christmas dinner with his family

He could not trap a mouse if it was eating off the same breakfast plate as he was . . .

—Jimmy Simpson,
referring to Tom Wilson

These cold nights turn thoughts of lonely bachelors to the problem of getting married or buying a coal oil heater.

—Banff *Crag and Canyon*, September 13, 1919

Do they talk about us in Hollywood? Do they know we're up here, or have they forgotten our existence?

—Actor Robert Mitchum,
on location in the Rockies
filming *The River of No Return* in 1953

See this world before the next one.

—Ad slogan used in early
CPR promotional posters

It's strange such a wet place should be so dry.

—"Bob" Edwards commenting in the
Banff *Crag and Canyon*, 1921,
on his first visit to the Cave & Basin
after taking twenty-five years to find it

Riding horseback a pillion may have looked picturesque in ye olden days, but it is inhumanity to both biped and quadruped for two people of the opposite sex to parade the streets these days perched on the quarter deck of a long-suffering cayuse, looks vulgar and is detrimental to dignity and—panties.

—Banff *Crag and Canyon*, July 5, 1919

I believe the alpine cow will lead to a marked improvement in the quality of the food served in lodgings in the Canadian Rockies.

—Sir Norman Watson, on his proposed
plan to raise cows north of Lake Louise

The villa lots will be "leased out to people of great wealth, who will erect handsome buildings upon them."

> —Prime Minister John A. Macdonald, predicting the future of Banff town site

The Rocky Mountain Hot Springs Reserve will undoubtedly "recoup the patients and recoup the treasury."

> —The Prime Minister again, this time commenting on the amazing qualities of the Sulfur Mountain hot springs

Tell the minister to imagine the money when thousands of cars start traveling through.

> —J. B. "Bunny" Harkin, Commissioner of National Parks, 1920, anticipating the impact of automobiles inside the national parks

I would rather stalk sheep than occupy a front seat in a heavenly choir.

> —Jimmy Simpson, guide and outfitter, on his passion for bighorn sheep hunting

They remind me of babes in the woods, and the sooner the robins come and cover them up with leaves the better . . .

> —A. O. Wheeler, president of the Canadian Alpine Club, complaining about the use of inexperienced eastern horse guides in the Rockies

Dat Chorcha, she vants to do too much.

> —Ernest Feuz, Swiss Guide, commenting on legendary climber Georgia Engelhard's enthusiasm for conquering peaks

With my close-cropped hair and fly-front pants, I was often rejected from Ladies Rooms or Beer Parlors where I was taken for a teen-age boy.

—Mountain climber Georgia Engelhard commenting on her atypical appearance for the times

. . . and I have no doubt that it will be a great watering place.

—John A. Macdonald, predicting Banff's
success as either a hot springs resort or
a great place to drink (we're not sure which)

YESTERDAY'S NEWS

A browse through old editions of the Banff *Crag and Canyon* provides a humorous glimpse of the good old days in the Rockies. Some things never seem to change.

Delights of Banff (1901)

Climbing Sulphur Mountain

Bathing in the Basin

Driving around the loop

A visit to the Buffalo park

A trip to the top of Tunnel Mountain

Visiting Geo. Fear's Curiosity Store

Riding a bucking horse

Riding one that won't buck

Walking in shady groves

Going to the depot in the evening

A visit to the Cave

Renting a cozy cottage

A visit to the government museum

Having a cooling drink at Charley Stenton's

A drive in one of Walter Fulmer's comfortable rigs

Catching a 9 lb. trout

John Walker's choice confectionery and fruits

Going to church

A visit to the Sign of the Goat Curio Store

A trip up the river on W. Mather's steam launch

A drive to Devil's Lake with Pete

Getting a "square" at the Hotel King Edward

A hot bath at the Grand View Villa

Morrison and Bradford's home-made bread

A trip on the tally-ho

The merry, merry maidens

Early Hot Springs Humour (1900)

SHEENY, IN OFFICE OF BATHING ESTABLISHMENT: "Give me von bath ticked blease."

CLERK: "There you are, sir."

SHEENY: "How much vas dot, my friend?"

CLERK: "One dollar, please."

SHEENY: "Vat! Von dollar for von bath?"

CLERK: "Yes, sir. Six for five dollars."

SHEENY: "Vell, dot vas scheaper alreatty; bud how do I know dot I vill liff for five years longer?"

Same Old Story? (1901)

During the past week the influx of visitors has been so large that accommodations have been taxed almost to the limit. What will it be like when Banff becomes the capital?

Banff, BC? (1908)

The official who is responsible for the address printed on the CPR Hotel key tags should secure a map of the Dominion and furbish his rusty geographic knowledge. The tags have the following address printed: "Banff Springs Hotel, Banff, BC." It is things like this that serve to confuse tourists, and indicate laxity of management on the part of officials.

A Typical Day in Banff (1907)

"Tabby" and the curio store bear engaged in a friendly tussle one evening this week, Pete proving too much for Tabby, who was laid out in a mud puddle. Tabby says he was going to have the suit cleaned anyway, so that the fall did not matter.

Wanted! News! (1959)

News is kind of skimpy in Anthracite these days,

what with everybody preparing for another monster tourist season, complete with trips to Carrot Crick. Our readers have let us down rather badly lately, and we therefore make this appeal:

"Don't hold out on us! If you have died, moved, eloped, been married, sold out, been gypped, bought a car, been born, caught a cold, been robbed, had a baby, been shot, been visiting, had company, stolen anything, cut a new tooth, been snake-bitten, bobbed your hair, learned to smoke, seen anything amusing, seen anything worth noting, tell us about it. We want news!"

A Tale of a Cat

At the Banff zoo the female cougar was housed next to the wolf cage. A visitor in 1935 happened upon the cougar cage at a rather strange moment: the neighbouring wolves had grabbed hold of her tail and were holding her firmly in place against the cage. The lioness screamed in pain as one of the wolves began to chew on the tail. The quick-thinking visitor grabbed a nearby hose, managing to force the wolves away with a blast of cold water. This is likely the only recorded incident of a human interfering in a fight between wolves and cougars (at least the only one in which the person was still alive to relay the story).

Déjà Vu? (1917)

To the tourist who visited Banff, say, twenty years ago, the Banff of today would seem a different spot—a different world. Then to the resident every tourist was known. Now, the average tourist passes through our gates and no one knows his coming or going, and he may be here today and gone tomorrow without arousing any local interest. The reason is not far to see. The tourist travel to Banff has developed and increased to such an extent that the town is about as cosmopolitan as any town of its size on the North American continent.

Oh, Deer! (1915)

An unfailing sign that the tourist season is about over is the presence of deer on the streets of Banff . . . The deer are not as profitable visitors as tourists, but they harmonize with the surrounding scenery a heap more than many of the latter. And when one is broke what's the odds. Let us have harmony in all things, darn the expense.

Bye Bye Mosquitoes!

In the summer of 1916, Dr. Gordon Hewitt, an entomologist from Ottawa, spent several days studying the habits of the "manners and ways of mosquitoes" in order to devise a scheme to reduce the number of skeeters, possibly eliminating them all together. The Parks Department was expected to act on his recommendations, reporting to the *Crag* that there is "no doubt Banffites and tourists will be comparatively free from the mosquito annoyance next season."

Local Gossip

"Local Gossip" (or "Local and General," "Local and Personal," or "Late Local News") was a regular feature in early editions of the *Crag and Canyon*. It featured a random listing of observations, comments, and goings-on in the Banff area. Here's a sample of some of the tidbits and insightful comments gleaned from columns between 1900 and 1920:

A car load of trout are to be placed in the streams of the park.

Milder weather.

A number of tourists made the discovery on Friday that showers in Banff contain considerable wetness.

The robins are with us once again. So are the cyclists.

A baby elk is one of the new exciting attractions at the animal enclosure.

Bill Peyto, guide and outfitter, has hung some very fine business cards around the hotels. Bill apparently intends on going into business.

No one is complaining of the cold today.

Banff is getting busier and busier, isn't it?

The paragraph in last week's paper as to the Irish Setter Rex having bit Miss Brewster, contained, we are assured, an inaccuracy; it was not Rex that did the biting, but another dog, and Mr. Gattley says Rex has never bit anyone.

Small flocks of ducks have lately been seen on the Bow River.

Some visitors saw two partridges in the bushes last week.

It is no child's play to run the Cave and Basin in the season.

Even in this warm weather some of our younger visitors need longer skirts.

The Chalet at Lake Louise is a dream and the Banff Springs Hotel is a nightmare.

Coyotes are reported to be fairly numerous close to town and there is more than one less rooster than there used to be.

A wild Canada goose has visited the captive ones in the cages at the Banff zoo.

A train load of sailors passed through Banff, west bound, Monday forenoon. They were a fine looking bunch of men.

There are two women in town who are absolutely clean. They walked up to the Upper Hot Springs last Sunday and spent the time limit in the bathing pool.

It should be understood that the mattress on the Bankhead rifle range was placed there for use of the club members when shooting, and not for other purposes.

Quite a number of hummingbirds have been observed in the village during the last few days.

More people want to see Sir Donald's head than knew of his existence when he was alive. (Sir Donald was the largest member of the bison herd at the buffalo paddock.)

The evening lullaby song about train time by the coyotes is much enjoyed by all who hear it.

Less than ¼ of visitors to Banff know how beautiful the Vermilion Lakes are by moonlight or at sunset.

The squirrels are the busiest little animals in the park just now.

A Banff woman was overheard telling a friend that she recently caught 14 fine trout on the railway track. Banff has always been noted for good fishing, but this is the first instance known of trout walking the ties to town to meet the angler half way.

The number of deer seen on Cave Avenue, together with the industry of the squirrels, would indicate old man winter is mooching along the Edmonton Trail.

Will Banffites toboggan this winter?

There is a story around town of a catch of trout in the Bow that came almost up to the limit. It is believed in some quarters that the catch was of the Bull variety, tut, tut.

Two tourists braved the blizzard Sunday afternoon and drove up to the Upper Hot Springs.

Bert Ashton reports standing room only at the Hot Springs Hotel.

Tom Wilson states he heard a bird singing in the St. Julien subdivision, on Tunnel Mountain, on Wednesday. But he neglected to state what kind of bird it was—Austrian or Hungarian.

10,550 visitors "washed themselves" at the Upper Hot Springs, and 22,732 at the Cave and Basin.

Automobiles are said to be scooting around the Park on forbidden trails. Last Sunday a joy wagon was noticed several miles up the Spray, and another got part way up to the Upper Hot Springs before it was turned back.

Owing to the frolics of a bevy of young men and maidens the other day, to the music of a mouth organ, the Parks Branch is seriously considering re-naming a well-known trail and calling it "Some Can-can" road.

A couple of deer inspected the toboggan slide Thursday.

The bicycle has taken the place of the cayuse in the affections of the younger boys in Banff.

Things we love to hate: the mosquito.

THE WILDERNESS ZONE

THE LAST OF THE SILLY QUESTIONS AND COMMENTS

Here's our last batch of visitor comments and questions, fresh out of the oven:

Is Lake Louise man-made?

Moraine Lake must be man-made. It looks like a big cat pushed boulders up against the end of it.

Is there more than just trees in Yoho?

What are the crowds like in Vancouver?

When do the trees grow?

You know, you have a beautiful country here. I just wish that when the US bought Alaska they had bought up the rest of Canada, too!

We had a talk with God on the way to Banff, but he didn't mention anything about rain.

Can you tell me what the peculiarities of Lake Louise are—if, indeed, it has any peculiarities?

Why does it rain here? It's sunny in Vancouver.

Wouldn't you say the weather's better now than it is later?

Will the waterfalls still have water in them by the time we get there?

When do you turn on the waterfalls?

When do they turn off Takakkaw Falls?

Are there any white people living in Newfoundland, or is it all just natives?

How many undiscovered lakes are there around here?

Does Lake Louise have tides?

Is sunrise in the morning?

What kind of tree is this lodgepole pine?

Does the line through the Canadian number 7 mean no numbers can follow it?

Is there more weather in Jasper than around here?

I took a picture of a tree when I was here thirteen years ago but I can't remember where it is. Can you tell me where to find it?

Can I see your copy of the *Native Trees of California*?

Why is the sun so warm?

Where is the thing you stick your finger in and feel around?

The Duke of Windsor never missed a chance to pee. He never knew when it might be his last. (Stated by a passing visitor.)

Do you have short ones or long ones?

Where are the mines where you can go panning for gold?

It's only recently that you Canadians began speaking English, isn't it?

Is the weather forecast under the sign that says weather?

The pollution in this park is similar to what I've experienced in New York and Los Angeles.

We're camped at Wilcox Creek campground and some time in the night the creek stopped. Is there a plumber working higher up on the creek?

What do you do if you're a lady?

Do you have green salads in Canada?

People are walking in all different directions on Banff Avenue. Is that an English custom?

Is the Spiral Tunnels a ride?

Do you go upside down in the Spiral Tunnels?

Can I hike through the Spiral Tunnels?

Do you have any information on veterinarian clinics in Eureka, California?

Can you give me a criminal pardon to enter the US?

How many trees are there in BC?

You Canadians don't believe in showers, do you?

Can you tell me the *exact* location of every alpine flower in the park?

Why don't you heat the glacial lakes so people can swim in them?

Where can I take my monkey for a walk?

In June and July, if you run out of real snow, do you make some so we can still ride our snowmobiles? (As asked by a Floridian.)

Why do they plant the trees so close together? They block the views of the mountains.

I guess it makes sense that lots of archeological sites are located near the highway. It would have been more convenient for them.

That's a lovely Canadian flag, does it come in other colours?

MOUNTAIN-GROWN CORN

I didn't write these jokes (okay, maybe one or two) so don't blame them on me, and don't send me nasty letters. I'm just reporting the facts as I know them. I *do* admit to using *some* of these jokes from time to time in talks, because, the sad thing is, they actually work.

How far south do the Canadian Rockies go? To the US border, of course.

Did you know there's not a single mosquito in the Rockies? They're all married and have big families.

How do you know when you've left Banff National Park? There's less development.

How do you stop a grizzly from charging? Take away its credit card.

Two hikers in the Rockies encounter a grizzly. One hiker calmly puts on a pair of sneakers, prompting his friend to yell, "What are you doing? You'll never outrun that bear!" To which the hiker replies, "I don't have to outrun the *bear*, I just have to outrun *you*."

How can you tell a grizzly bear from a black bear? The grizzly will knock over the tree to get you; the black bear will climb up after you.

Two wardens investigate a bear mauling. A Czechoslovakian camper has been eaten. They interview witnesses to the horrific event and discover the poor fellow was eaten by a large male grizzly. "Are you *certain* it was a male?" "Yes, yes," the witnesses reply. Armed with this knowledge, the wardens track and eventually kill the male grizzly. They cut open the bear but find no remains of the camper. It eventually turns out that it was not a male bear, but a large female that ate the hapless camper. Which just goes to show, you can never believe anyone when they say, "The Czech's in the male."

Overheard in Banff National Park: "Yes folks, we now ship all our garbage back to Calgary—where it came from in the first place."

In 1950 Princess Elizabeth and Philip, the Duke of Edinburgh, visited the Canadian Rockies. They were watching buffalo at a salt lick, when Philip piped up with, "What's the difference between a bison and a buffalo?" Before an answer could be given, Philip answered his own question: "Oh, I think I know," he grinned. "A bison is what the Australians use to wash in."

How deep is Lake Louise? Well, it goes all the way to the bottom.

Maligne Lake is a drown-proof lake. You'll freeze to death long before you drown.

How many people work for Parks Canada? About half.

How do porcupines mate? Very carefully.*

Why did the chicken cross the road? To show the porcupine it could be done.

Do you know what Banff stands for? Be Aware Nothing For Free.

How many wardens does it take to clean up a road kill? Depends how hungry they are.

IMPRACTICAL PRACTICAL JOKES IN THE ROCKIES

The most often-played practical joke in the mountains is quite silly, yet surprisingly effective. It involves sneaking rocks, beer, car jacks, anvils, or anything else of substantial weight into your buddy's backpack just before a grueling hike. If you're going along, of course, the best thing to put in his pack is wine or beer, because then you get to benefit from drinking it *and* you get to enjoy the conversation, which generally goes like this:

---

* This may no longer be funny, if it ever was, but plain true, according to an article in *New Scientist* magazine. Rick Sweitzer of the University of California and Joel Berger at the University of Nevada reported that a five-year study proved once and for all that porcupines *do* mate very carefully. The females got spiked "only rarely" over the five-year period. They also discovered that quills serve as sexual display as much as they do for protection. The females, it seems, go for the porcupines with the biggest quills.

You (the clever practical joker): Whew, what a slog those last twenty-three kilometres were. Made the first sixteen look like a cakewalk. How about some beer now?

Unsuspecting Friend: What? Were you stupid enough to pack beer all the way up here?

You: No. *You* were.

You'll be a giggling pile of jelly as your friend empties his pack. You'll laugh even harder when he hauls out the beer, and as he grabs the nearest rock and attempts to bludgeon you to death, you'll be damned near peeing your pants. Ah, fun in the mountains—it doesn't get much better than this.

Aqua Court Gold

It was immature, juvenile, silly, and a little disgusting —in other words, just what you'd expect from a group of young naturalists. The target of the prank were swimmers at the Radium Hot Springs. The pranksters covered Douglas fir cones in a mixture of peanut butter and cocoa, then had an inside man release them strategically from the bottom of the pool. Some of the cones floated, others sank, but *all* of them produced the desired effect. Mothers grabbed their children. Children either laughed or screamed. At one

A woman reacts to spotting "mystery" debris floating in the hot springs.
Whyte Museum of the Canadian Rockies/ NA-66-1910

end of the pool, two elderly ladies delicately made waves with their hands in an effort to "shoo" the mystery objects away. And the poor lifeguards donned gloves and grabbed their longest dip nets in an effort to remove the "toxic waste" from the pool. Because the guards looked as if they were skimming for gold, the floating debris became known as "aqua court gold."

Kootenay's Angels

People who know Kootenay National Park's beloved Larry Halverson know he's not the type to instill fear in anyone's heart—not even when he tries. One day Larry and a buddy decided to dress up as tough, dangerous-looking bikers and ride into the dusty little town of Field on a tiny Honda. When they pulled up to the Yoho National Park administration building they tried to look as cool and menacing as possible. Tripping on the sissy bar and falling over each other didn't give them the edge they were looking for, but they sauntered into the administration building anyway, wearing intimidating scowls and carrying heavy chains (assuming that bikers take their chains with them everywhere). The receptionist did not look amused. They explained they were up from New York and Chicago.

"We want to book a group campsite for 300 of our buddies for ten days," they said.

"You'll have to take the chains outside," replied the receptionist.

Larry and his buddy regarded each other in silence. "They're for winter travel," one of them said. "We thought there'd be snow in Canada."

She didn't buy it. The chains went outside.

"And for what purpose do you want a group campground?" she asked.

"Ah, you know, to listen to some music, hang out with some buds, commune with nature . . ."

The receptionist still didn't look amused. She looked even less amused when the park superintendent emerged from his office, took one look at the bikers, and disappeared quietly down the back stairs, leaving her to fend for herself.

The gag finally ended when, in Larry's own words, he and his buddy "took off our helmets and exposed ourselves." (I'm not really sure how that would have helped the situation.)

A Howling Time at Whistlers

Park naturalists decided to give campers at Whistlers Campground in Jasper an unforgettable wilderness experience. At 2:00 AM one summer morning they played a tape of wolves howling over the theatre PA system—loud enough so howling wolves were heard for miles around. The next morning Parks Canada was inundated with reports of the *canis lupus* symphony. The illusion delighted campers so much, the jokers thought about dressing up as bears for the following evening's entertainment, but decided against it for safety reasons.

An Investment in Education

This isn't so much a practical joke as an easy way to line one's pocket. It's an old trick used by seasoned naturalists on guided hikes. You simply plant a co-conspirator in the back of the audience. On completion of the walk, your helpful associate reaches forward with a smile on his face and a ten-dollar bill in his hand and announces in a loud voice, "Thanks, that was a great hike." Before long everyone is dipping into their pockets and you, innocent park naturalist that you are, have pocketed several hundred dollars toward your winter vacation in Costa Rica.

Warning: this was only done back in the old days when no one paid for these services. To attempt such a subterfuge today would be foolhardy and dangerous.

Caution: Elephant Crossing

A few years ago a large sign warned visitors driving up the Kootenay Parkway to watch for red elephants. It was April 1st, naturally, and the cut-out elephant sign appeared where a large elk sign normally

Motorists along the Kootenay Parkway are
advised to keep a sharp eye out for red
elephants. *Michael Kerr*

greeted drivers. The scary part of this story is the number of red elephant sightings recorded by visitors throughout the mountains that day.

Deer in the Headlamp

A local fellow was quite shocked one evening when he ventured out to his van in search of more beer. In order to guide his way, he donned his headlamp. (It's a Canadian mountain tradition, using a headlamp to search for beer in the dark.) He was rummaging around in back of the van when a shadow caught his eye. There seemed to be something rather large sitting in the driver's seat. He approached cautiously. His pulse quickened. Then the light from his headlamp revealed the mystery object. It was a deer, propped in a sitting position with its hooves tied to the steering wheel. Some Parks Canada comedians, after sadly picking the deer up off the highway, had decided to pull a fast one. The victim of the joke probably wondered whether he really needed that last beer or not.

SATURDAY NIGHT BEAVER

Let's clear this up at the outset: giardia is *not* our friend. Giardia—properly called *giardia lamblia* (although if you do call it, it probably won't respond)—is a protozoan parasite that lives in many Rocky Mountain waterways. Beavers, dogs, and horses are all known to spread it, though the beaver gets the brunt of the blame for some reason. People who drink water infected with the parasite will sometimes get what is commonly known as *beaver fever*. The symptoms include diarrhoea, gas, cramps, lack of appetite, a compelling urge to watch reruns of *Leave it to Beaver*, sexual arousal at the sound of running water, and a desire to listen to old ABBA songs. (Some people—admittedly few—have expressed a desire to listen to Neil Diamond songs.)

Beaver fever is not the only nickname for this unfortunate condition, as this authoritative listing of the euphemisms and folk names for this tenacious bug will attest:

Night of the Killer Beaver

Rambo IV

A Bad Case of the Trilobites

The I-Wish-I-Still-Had-My-ABBA-Collection Syndrome

Saturday Night Beaver

The Rodent's Revenge

The Macarena from Hell

Leave it to that Damned Beaver

Bucky's Big Night Out

Mountain Madness Closing Out Sale

The I-Wish-I-Owned-a-Trapline Disease

The Furball Express

THE JURASSIC PARK CATTLE GUARD

Visitors often (okay, maybe not often, but at least twice)

ask if there are cows in Banff National Park. They ask because of our cattle guards, also known as Texas gates. Of course we don't have cows, but we do have wildlife that we try to keep off the highway with fences and cattle guards. We also have one rather infamous cattle guard located at the entrance to the beautiful Parks Canada administration building in the town of Banff. It's designed to keep elk from feasting on the Cascade Garden salad bar on the grounds of the building. It's infamous because it was designed with the same specifications used at Jurassic Park to keep dinosaurs from wandering off the grounds. Yes, it's big—so big it makes an ordinary Texas gate look like a barbecue grill, so big even the CPR wouldn't locate a railway route over it. It's so big . . . well, you get the picture. So, in honour of the biggest Texas gate this side of Texas, here are

The Top Ten Things That Can't Cross the Banff Administration Building Cattle Guard

10. Tyrannosaurus Rex
9. Kangaroos
8. Men wearing high heels (I only tried it once, honest.)

A park visitor attempts to navigate the Jurassic Park cattleguard.
Michael Kerr

7. Water buffalo (Although water buffalo don't frequent the park, it is a comfort to know we could seek refuge in the administration building if they did show up.)

6. Most foreign cars

5. Most domestic cars

4. Chinook winds

3. That monster dump truck (it's the biggest in the world!) from Sparwood, BC

2. Migrating salmon

1. Elvis (the later years)

SEX IN THE ROCKIES

Sex in the Rockies is different from, say, sex under water. For starters, because of the steep terrain, it's difficult to find level ground (if you're into that sort of boring, mundane sex). You also have wildlife to contend with, many of whom are also trying to have sex. And then there are the ever-observant eyes of the park wardens, who are always looking (and, if the truth be known, hoping) to catch people in the act. They claim it's research, but I don't buy it.

In my on-going attempt to be helpful, here are ten things you should know before engaging in sex in the Rockies:

1. Sex in national parks is, thank goodness, considered "an appropriate use," and is thus tolerated to a degree, depending on the nature of the act. It is clearly referred to in the National Park Dedication Clause, where we read: "National parks are dedicated for the enjoyment of future generations."

2. Always practice safe sex in the mountains. If you're climbing, rope up. If you're in a canoe, keep your lifejacket on, and for goodness' sake always use a condom—the mosquitoes are terrible.

3. When having sex while camping, make lots of noise.

This will not only keep the bears away, but it will drown out the noise of your fellow campers having sex. This, of course, may attract a male moose during the mating season, but it's probably worth the risk.

4. When in a camper, trailer, or small RV, keep in mind that the shock absorbers are not *that* good. We all know what's going on in there.

5. Don't have sex in any of the hot springs; it's been done to death.

6. During sex, keep your park permit fastened on a string around your neck in case a warden insists on seeing it. They may not have checked it at the gates, or in the campground, or on a hiking trail, but now, for some reason, they will definitely need to see it.

7. Do not use whipped cream or other body flavouring additives when in bear country, as this will attract pretty much every bear within a 500-kilometre radius.

8. Do not engage in sexual activities within 100 metres of a national park roadway, as this will create a "sex jam," which is far more dangerous than the worst bear jam you can imagine.

9. Most locals are familiar with what constitutes legitimate climbing gear, so be careful trying to pass off your bondage accoutrements as "the mountain climber's essentials."

10. Do not engage in sexual activities with Boomer the Beaver, no matter how persistent he may be.

THE CHINOOK MADE ME DO IT

The weather in the Rockies changes more often than park entrance fees. And, to really throw an open umbrella into the thick of things, we get a taste of winter every summer and a taste of summer every winter.

Invariably, in the middle of August—or, according to weather stats, any time during the summer—we are treated to a snowfall in many parts of the mountains. This scares the hell out of our guests from Florida. If you're a true Canadian, however, you simply strap on the snowshoes and trudge off to work as though it were any other day. If you're a Columbian ground squirrel hanging out by the Lake Louise Inn, you do the only sensible thing: you pack things in and go into hibernation for the year.

The taste of summer in winter is much more welcome, and comes in the nicely packaged form of chinooks. Chinooks are warm, westerly winds that swoop out of the mountains and provide a nice little gift for Calgarians and most mountain communities on the eastern slopes. They happen year-round, but we tend only to feel them during the winter. The temperature can rise as much as 30°C (that's Canadian, not American degrees) in a few short hours (actually, the hours are as long as any—sixty minutes each).

Chinooks affect our moods much the way thunderstorms do. The changing atmospheric pressure and the sudden imbalance of ions in the air can play havoc with our hormones. Thus, chinooks are associated with mood swings, which account for a lot of cranky Canadians in the middle of winter. (Waterton is in a constant state of chinook, so they are *always* a little cranky down there.) Chinooks are also linked to a rise in automobile accidents, increased instances of people listening to old Perry Como records, and even a jump in crime.

The rise in crime rates is easy to explain and has nothing to do with people going wacko because of the weather. It has simply to do with the fact that no sane criminal is going to rob a bank when it's -40°C outside. Fingers are too numb to hold a gun steady, getaway cars invariably need a boost, and *everyone* is wearing a ski mask. Thus, like the rest of us, they

A windy event that takes place on the other side of the Great Divide is known as the Yoho Blow, a cold wind that whistles down the Yoho Valley and over the little town of Field. I mention this only because for the longest time I thought a Yoho Blow was something entirely different, but we won't go there.

If you're looking for current information on the weather in the Rockies, phone 1-800-WHOKNOWS. The message is updated every five minutes.

wait for a nice warm chinook to go about their business.

From Our "Back on This Day in the Weather" Files

Edward Whymper, a climber (the "Conqueror of the Matterhorn") was hired in 1901 by the CPR to look into the possibilities of making their resorts in the Rockies more popular. I'm not sure he succeeded. Arriving in Lake Louise during the second week of July, he referred to the days of the week as follows: Stormday, Rainday, Mistday, Hailday, Thunderday, Snow-day, and Sleetday.

And as recorded in the Glacier House log book from a climber in the Selkirks*

First it rained, and then it snew,
and then it friz and then it thew,
and then it fogged, and then it blew,
and very shortly after then,
it rained and snew
and friz and thew

and fogged and
blew
again.

AN ELMER FUDD THEME PARK?

There's been a lot
of debate about the
level of develop-
ment in Banff.
Some say Banff
should keep grow-
ing, some say it
should be man-
aged like a national
park, while others
say scrap the whole
thing and put up an
Elmer Fudd Theme
Park. Still others,
even sillier, say we
should find out if
overcrowding is
keeping visitors

A tourist narrowly survives an encounter with a grizzly bear. *Claudine Dumais*

A tourist narrowly survives a shopping trip along Banff Avenue. *Claudine Dumais*

away, because if we knew this we could market more
effectively and get more visitors. This is known as the
chicken-and-egg marketing strategy.

There *do* seem to be some disconcerting signs that,
like Pamela Anderson, Banff may be just a little *too*
developed for its own good.

---

* I know, the Selkirks aren't in the Rockies, but this is cute, it pertains to mountain weather, and it's the only place the Columbia Mountains (who take
themselves far too seriously, compared to the Rockies) appear in the book.

Signs that Banff Has Gone a Tad Too Far

Donald Trump seen walking into local real estate office.

Cascade Mountain is no longer the biggest landmark in the area.

Only fossils left seen drinking coffee in local cafes.

Elk have begun applying for low-income housing.

Local climbers setting sights on latest shopping mall as their next ascent.

Takes nearly twenty minutes to see an elk now.

The only signs of wildlife are the street signs at the corner of Moose and Grizzly.

One more storey on the next mall and Banff will beat out Lake Louise as the highest community in Canada.

New Yorkers avoid the place because it's too crowded.

IS THAT A HAIRY CHESTED NUT-SCRATCHER?

I've always thought statues should say something. You

The Van Horne statue welcomes guests to the famous Banff Springs Hotel. What he is pointing at remains a mystery. *Michael Kerr*

should be able to pull a string and activate a taped message. Or they could have a balloon coming out of their mouths, like a comic book character. Some might suggest this is rather tasteless, so we won't think about them right now.

A rather imposing statue welcomes visitors to the historic Banff Springs Hotel in Banff. It's of William Cornelius Van Horne, the general manager of the CPR. He's famous for the line, "If we can't export the scenery, we'll have to import the tourists." I don't think that's what his statue is saying, though. If it were, he wouldn't be pointing; he'd be rubbing his hands together, dreaming of all the money he'd be making once those tourists started to arrive. My guess is Van Horne is actually saying one of the following lines:

> Go back—you can't even *think* about affording this place!
>
> You in the green shorts and brown sneakers—get a haircut.
>
> That bird over there—is that a hairy chested nutscratcher?
>
> Go east, young man—you'll find plenty of parking *there*!
>
> Go downtown and shop your assess off. NOW!
>
> Look, it's Elvis!
>
> Ha, ha! Made you look!
>
> Get that motor home out of here! Can't you see this is no place for people like you?

HOLLYWOOD COMES TO THE ROCKIES

> *QUESTION:* What two famous blondes have gone over the Bow River Falls in Banff National Park?
> *ANSWER:* Marilyn Monroe and Laddie (the son of Lassie).

Laddie was the first to swim the falls—in the 1945 movie *Son of Lassie*, starring Peter Lawford. While attempting to elude the Nazis during World War II, Laddie is swept up into his master's arms, who then leaps off the Stewart Canyon bridge (in our world, found along the Lake Minnewanka trail), ending up in the tumultuous waters below the Bow Falls. Of course, they escape the Nazis. Now, if only Laddie could escape his moronic owner . . .

Marilyn did it on a raft with Robert Mitchum in the 1954 *River of No Return*. Perhaps I should rephrase that last sentence: Marilyn *went over the falls* with Mitchum (get your minds out of the gutter). The special effects in this little gem leave much to be desired. Marilyn looks a lot like a Barbie doll splashing around in a Jacuzzi.

Marilyn Monroe and Robert Mitchum prepare to navigate the Bow Falls (really, kids, this is the only safe way to do it).
Whyte Museum of the Canadian Rockies/NA-66-1679

These are only two of the many Hollywood movies that have been filmed in the Canadian Rockies. With scenery like ours for a backdrop, it's no wonder we've hosted some seventy-odd films in the area. (And believe me, some of them were very odd, indeed). If you think silly things happen when your average visitor encounters the wilds of Canada, imagine Hollywood trying to make silly things happen on top of silly things already happening.

In the name of Hollywood, people have live-trapped wolverines, blown up a cabin on the shore of Moraine Lake, and dumped buckets of lemmings into the Bow River. (Contrary to popular myth, the lemmings did not, and do not, choose these mass cult suicides on their own.) So, in honour of the silliness that prevails when Hollywood comes for a visit, I now present . . . The Canadian Rocky Oscars Winners (aka The Crows):

Most Unlikely Film Made in the Rockies

Saskatchewan (1954) starring Alan Ladd and Shelley Winters.

Quickest Walk in the Rockies

In one short scene in *Son of Lassie*, Peter Lawford manages to traverse the shores of Moraine Lake and Lake Louise, and then take in the meadows of Bow Summit high above Peyto Lake—all in just a few steps.

Best (and Briefest) Set Design

Superman II (1980) in which the Athabasca Glacier in Jasper is made to look like the North Pole for Superman's trip to his Fortress of Solitude. The scene is five seconds long.

Film Least Likely to Be Screened at Local Ski Hills

Ski Lift to Death (1978). The video release is titled *Snowblind*, which would be the preferred state for anyone watching this movie.

Worst Film Ever Made in the Rockies

Ski Lift to Death (1978). Disco era, ski ballet, bad acting, gondola hanging from a thread—you do the math.

When Hollywood comes to the Rockies,
things can get a little strange.
Whyte Museum of the Canadian Rockies/NA-66-1691

Most Rocky Mountainish Ending

Eternal Love (1928). This silent picture finds two star-crossed lovers dying in each others' arms in an avalanche off Mount Victoria.

Best Film Not-Really-Made-Here-Though-Everyone-Thinks-It-Was

Doctor Zhivago (1965). Only a few seconds of actual Rockies scenery—all from the Yoho area—appear in this film.

Only Film In Which Anthony Hopkins Gets To Kill a Grizzly

The Edge (1997). Originally, it was called *Bookworm*, but producers felt that would be an unlikely name for a movie in which a grizzly gets killed.

Best Nickname for a Rockies Movie

The River of No Return was dubbed "The Picture of No Return" by Robert Mitchum, who wondered if the film would ever get made, and if anyone in Hollywood knew he was still alive.

The First Film Made in the Rockies

Under the Top (1919) features a scene of a car being swept over the Bow Falls. (It seems that things are always going over the falls, doesn't it?)

Best Use of a Famous Rocky Mountain Landmark

Last of the Dogmen (1994). The "Dogmen" are hiding in a valley that one can access only by going through a natural tunnel strategically hidden behind the Takakkaw Waterfalls in Yoho National Park.

Film That Got the Most Number of Local Women Excited

Legends of the Fall (1993), starring Brad Pitt, Anthony Hopkins, and Aidan Quinn, all of whom were rumoured to be camping in the Rockies.

Only Film Made in the Area That Actually Won the Oscar for Best Picture

Unforgiven (1991), starring and directed by Clint Eastwood. Rumour has it Clint would have shot all the members of the Academy if they hadn't awarded this film the Oscar.

Film That Most Sounds Like a Cheap Porno Flick

The Love Master (1924), is really about a German shepherd named Strongheart. Apparently, there's still a line of dog food in the United States named after this canine.

Most Jealous Celebrity

Elle Macpherson from *The Edge*. The target of her jealousy? Her 1,300-pound co-star, Bart the bear: "Bart was paid more than me, and he was equipped for the Alberta fall weather. I had to do several of my scenes in freezing weather wearing the skimpiest costumes." Bart's fee, incidentally, came in at one million dollars.

Most Improbable Event Portrayed in a Rockies Film

Forty Ninth Parallel (1940) was a film about Nazis on the run who somehow manage to take a much-needed break and take part in the Banff Indian Days celebrations.

Most Deserving Oscar Winner for Best Cinematography

Legends of the Fall took the Oscar in this category— thanks, of course, to those stunning Rocky Mountains that make even mediocre films at least *look* good.

Star With the Smelliest Breath

Bart the bear takes the honours for his dramatic portrayal of a grizzly experiencing mid-life angst and rage in the thriller, *The Edge*. As Bart's bigger-than-life co-star Anthony Hopkins explained, "He smelt of garlic because he eats pasta and chicken before each scene." Bart, you see, although getting a hefty fee, works for chicken feed. Actually, he works for the chickens themselves, and apparently he's an eight-chicken star. The grizzly refuses to work after his eighth bird.

Lousiest Wilderness Tips Delivered in a Movie

Despite portraying an extremely intelligent and well-read character, Anthony Hopkin's character in *The Edge* offers up some seriously lousy advice for folks venturing into the mountains. Rather than using flares to signal search planes, our heroes use them to start a campfire. Rather than using the sun to help guide their way, they opt for the old paper clip in the water routine. And despite the fact that the innkeeper at the start of the film warned everyone to remain still if they encountered a bear, the two numbskulls run for their lives every time they meet up with Bart, the infamous man-eating grizzly.

The Rockies have rarely played themselves. They are, in fact, masters of disguise, having played nearly everywhere *but* the Canadian Rockies. Here's a rundown of some of the roles these beauties have played:

Alaska	Russia
Wyoming	Oklahoma
The Swiss Alps	Austria
Norway	Czechoslovakia
Montana	Yukon
The Japanese Alps	Saskatchewan

Question: What two large, male celebrities have co-starred in two films made in the Canadian Rockies?

Answer: Bart, the bear, and Anthony Hopkins, the man, each co-starred in *Legends of the Fall* and *The Edge*.

In the movie *The Edge*, the closing credits include one Brian Steele. His job? "Double for the Bear," of course. We can only assume Brian is one hairy fellow.

Best Comedy Disguised as a Drama

Once again, the honours go to *The Edge*. I laughed so hard I thought I'd cry.

TEN REASONS WATERTON LAKES ISN'T MENTIONED MORE OFTEN IN THIS BOOK

10. Where?

9. Watertonites are too cranky because of the frequent chinooks.

8. Proximity to the States has sucked some of the fun out of them.

7. Proximity to the prairies has sucked the remaining fun out of them.

6. International Peace Park designation has gone to their heads.

5. Recent designation as a World Heritage Site has put a stop to their continuous giggling and immature hijinks.

4. Too far to drive for good stories.

3. They've been cut off from all outside communications owing to recent invasion by the United States.

2. They're afraid someone will find out they're secretly running a nudist colony.

1. They're too embarrassed to be mentioned in the same book as Banff.

AND NOW, THE NEWS . . .

Here are a few headlines that may make you want to read just a little more about our beloved Canadian Rockies:

Tourists Thought They Could Subdue Grizzly
With Love
—Calgary *Herald*, September 29, 1995

Animals Responsible for Shortage of Wardens
—Banff *Crag and Canyon*, August 4, 1988

Cow Moose Stops for Red Light Then Heads
Up Main
—Jasper *Totem*, September 26, 1962

Stop and Go Lights for Banff Elk
—Banff *Crag and Canyon*, December 8, 1944

Theatre Employee Dives Into Empty Pool after
Basin is Closed
—Banff *Crag and Canyon*, August 11, 1944

New Wardens Do Their "Dances With Elk"
—Banff *Crag and Canyon*, February 19, 1992

Marmot Being Groomed
—Jasper *Booster*, July 22, 1970

Don't Need Guide for Guided Tour
—Jasper *Booster*, August 12, 1970

Animals Moving Into Town
—Jasper *Booster*, September 12, 1973

More Bears or People? A Hard One to Answer
—Banff *Crag and Canyon*, July 19, 1978

Jasper National Park—A Tourist Attraction?
—Jasper *Booster*, June 19, 1974

Jasper Bears Minding Their Manners for Summer
Guests
—Jasper *Booster*, August 10, 1994

Banff Should Be a Pleasant Place
—Jasper *Booster*, July 23, 1975

Is There Life After Jasper?
—Jasper *Booster*, November 21, 1984

Bull Elk Becoming Modest
—Banff *Crag and Canyon*, August 2, 1935

Memo to Parks: Be Reasonable!
—Jasper *Booster*, May 22, 1996

Mace-Toting Granny Offered Better Show of Hospitality
—Banff *Crag and Canyon*, September 9, 1993

Cow Elk are Getting Into Annual Fall Rampage
—Jasper *Booster*, July 13, 1994

The Bear Facts? Well, He Liked Our Lunch
—Banff *Crag and Canyon*, August 28, 1996

Munching Pair of Deer a Menace
—Jasper *Booster*, August 9, 1989

Even the Bears Have Been Confused by the Weather
—Jasper *Booster*, February 3, 1993

Wardens Do It for Real
—Jasper *Booster*, January 31, 1996

Bear Burgles Bakery
—Banff *Crag and Canyon*, October 7, 1992

Elk Cows Ready for the Tourist Tango
—Jasper *Booster*, May 19, 1993

Hibernating Ground Squirrels Won't Delay Co-op Project
—Jasper *Booster*, November 9, 1994

Bears Get Official Nod to Sleep In
—Jasper *Booster*, March 31, 1993

Santa Wants Our Elk!
—Jasper *Booster*, December 25, 1996

You're Never Too Old to Dress Up in a Goofy Costume*
—Jasper *Booster*, October 26, 1994

Jasper Elk Staying Remarkably Mellow
—Jasper *Booster*, June 20, 1993

Bear Bites Park Superintendent
—Banff *Crag and Canyon*, June 29, 1977

---

* I know, this isn't a very mountainish theme. I just like it because of its timely and important message.

Repeat Elk Offender Gets Solitary Sentence
—Jasper *Booster*, June 2, 1993

Wardens Study Female Deer With Antlers
—Banff *Crag and Canyon*, December 12, 1990

Remember How Funny Winter Was?
—Jasper *Booster*, October 15, 1996

Scientist Dons Antlers to Study Moose Mating Habits
—Banff *Crag and Canyon*, August 26, 1987

Parks Canada Sees the Light
—Jasper *Booster*, November 13, 1996

THE GREAT CANADIAN ROCKIES QUIZ

Do **You Canadians Know Anything?**

1. How far south do the Canadian Rockies go?
2. How do you get to Jasper from where you are right now?
    A) Turn left then head straight
    B) You can't get there from there
    C) Why would you?
3. The official symbol of Parks Canada is:
    A) Snoopy
    B) A pork chop
    C) A beaver
    D) In dire need of a facelift
    E) All of the above
4. What's the difference between a moose?
5. At what elevation does an elk become a moose?
    A) 3,500 metres
    B) You can't really become a moose; you can only try to imagine what it would be like to be similar to a moose
    C) Depends on El Niño

6. How can you tell the difference between a big-horn sheep and a mountain goat?
   A) You can't—not from here, anyway
   B) The sheep are hornier; the goats are the long-hairs
   C) The sheep are always seen in close proximity to park wardens

7. What should you do if you encounter a bear?
   A) Put on your sneakers
   B) Climb the nearest tall person
   C) Squeal like a pig
   D) Play "partially wounded" to elicit empathy
   E) Don't get in a car with it

8. The Rockies are named the Rockies because, excluding *Rocky IV*, it's where all the Rocky movies were filmed. True or False?

9. If you get lost while hiking in the backcountry of the Rocky Mountains . . .
   A) It's too bad; we'll miss you
   B) No one will come looking for you because we're still mad at you
   C) You're pretty much screwed

10. You're park permit pays for:
    A) Entrance to all future Rolling Stones concerts
    B) The oxygen you'll be breathing while in the park
    C) The cost of manufacturing the permit itself

11. Bear pepper spray should be used:
    A) Only into a heavy wind
    B) On your underarms to keep bears at bay
    C) On your backcountry pasta dish to add a little flavouring

12. Banff was declared a national park in:
    A) 1492
    B) Both official languages

C) Case there was nowhere else to put the Trans-Canada Highway

D) Hopes of reviving a sagging T-shirt industry

13. The highest mountain in the Canadian Rockies is:

A) Higher than your house

B) Higher than other mountains in the Canadian Rockies

C) Pretty darn high

14. Park wardens sometimes set areas of the park on fire because:

A) They feel like it

B) They're cold

C) They enjoy a good weenie roast as much as the next guy

D) They're not allowed to burn areas outside the park

15. The best way to remove a wood tick from your body is:

A) Have the body part amputated

B) Douse yourself in gasoline, then attend the next controlled burn

C) Ask that cute girl in apartment 4-C to do it

D) Ask that cute guy in apartment 5-B to do it

16. If you're going to have sex in the Canadian Rockies . . .

A) For goodness' sake, don't tell us about it

B) Contact the nearest warden office for a permit

C) Yeah, right. Like you'll ever have sex in this millennium

17. Boomer the Beaver is:

A) The bouncer at your local bar

B) Wanted in thirty-two states and seven provinces

C) The nickname for a crazed beaver that went on a rampage in the early 70s, toppling three seniors with wooden legs

18. You should avoid the elk in Banff town because:
    A) They've been avoiding you
    B) They have bad breath
    C) You have an IQ that is actually measurable

19. Giardia is:
    A) Not our friend
    B) The name of a Latin American dance
    C) What the restaurant will explain you have in response to your food poisoning complaint

20. If you see a mountain shaped like Elvis, you should:
    A) Take a photograph and send it to the Prime Minister
    B) Seek professional help
    C) Climb to the top so you can tell people you sat on Elvis

21. The Canadian Rockies are special because:
    A) They're pretty big, compared to, say, Saskatoon
    B) It's where you caught your first sexually transmitted disease
    C) They go all the way to the US border

A FIELD GUIDE TO
ROCKY MOUNTAIN HUMOUR - LIVE!

Introducing the live, stand-up, in-person-and-in-your-face version of *When Do You Let the Animals Out?* If you loved the book, why not make Michael Kerr a part of your next conference, incentive group, team-building session, family outing, corporate retreat, corporate attack, or "well, here we all are" gathering?

Yes, folks, it's a live program based on this book that includes the very best of Rocky Mountain Humour featuring the twenty-five silliest visitor questions of all time, amusing anecdotes, wacky costumes, valuable prizes (okay, so they're not all that valuable, but you know you'll want one anyway), and even some useful information about this place we call the Rocky Mountains. The live version of *When Do You Let the Animals Out?* is the perfect way to kick off or wind down your stay in the Canadian Rockies.

Program Highlights Include:

Out of the Mouths of Park Visitors
Unbearable Bear Stories

Tales of Tails and Other Stories
The Hysterical History of the Rockies

The Great Canadian Rockies Quiz
and much, much more!

For more information or to make a booking, contact:

Michael Kerr
Speaking of Ideas
Phone/Fax: (403) 609-2640
e-mail: mkerr@banff.net
322 Canyon Close
Canmore, Alberta
T1W 1H4